## About the Authors

JAMES THURBER (1894–1961) was a staff member at *The New Yorker* for more than thirty years, where his humorous drawings and "Talk of the Town" columns made him famous. His many published works include *My Life and Hard Times*, *My World—and Welcome to It*, *The Years with Ross*, and the children's book *Many Moons*, which won a Caldecott Award.

E. B. WHITE (1899–1985) began his career as a contributor to *The New Yorker* in 1925, joining the staff in 1927. He is widely known as the author of two children's classics, *Charlotte's Web* and *Stuart Little*, as well as one of the finest essayists of the twentieth century, many of which are collected in *Essays of E. B. White* and *Writings from "The New Yorker" 1927–1976*.

# IS SEX NECESSARY?

# IS SEX NECESSARY?

## OR

## Why You Feel the Way You Do

By

## JAMES THURBER & E. B. WHITE

with an introduction by

### E. B. WHITE

Foreword by John Updike

## Perennial

*An Imprint of HarperCollinsPublishers*

First Perennial edition published 2004.

Library of Congress Cataloging-in-Publication Data
Thurber, James, 1894–1961.
    Is sex necessary? or, Why you feel the way you do / by James Thurber & E.B. White ; with an introduction by E.B. White ; foreword by John Updike.
      p.  cm.
    ISBN 0-06-073314-4
    1. Sex—Humor.  I. Title: Is sex necessary?.  II. Title: Why you feel the way you do.  III. White, E. B. (Elwyn Brooks), 1899–  IV. Title.

    PS3539.H94I8 2004
    818'.5207—dc22

                                         2004051099

04 05 06 07 08 RRDH 10 9 8 7 6 5 4 3 2 1

TO DAISY AND JEANIE

"Things look pretty bad right now"
       —MAJ. GEN. BRIGGS, AT SHILOH

ANY reader who has already
begun to be confused by the
drawings in this book should
turn to Page 178, where they
are explained.

# CONTENTS

# FOREWORD TO
# THE PERENNIAL EDITION

FOR some years, including the months of 1929 when they jointly composed *Is Sex Necessary?*, James Thurber and E. B. White shared, during office hours, a small room at *The New Yorker*. White had already become the darling of the magazine's editor, Harold Ross; it was through White's suggestion, in 1927, that Ross had hired Thurber, who at the age of thirty-two was still a struggling writer from Columbus, Ohio, with little to show for several journalistic stints and aspiring sojourns in Manhattan and Paris. While they shared their close quarters, White tutored Thurber in the art of writing for "Talk of the Town," and Thurber gradually became the chief "Talk" writer and rewrite man. When Thurber died in 1961, White remembered the period fondly:

> It was a fine thing to be young and at work in New York for a new magazine when Thurber was young and at work, and I will always be glad that this happened to me.

It was fortunate that we got on well; the office we shared was the size of a hall bedroom. There was just room enough for two men, two typewriters, and a stack of copy paper. The copy paper disappeared at a scandalous rate—not because our production was high (although it was) but because Thurber used copy paper as the natural receptacle for discarded sorrow, immediate joys, stale dreams, golden prophecies, and messages of good cheer to the outside world and to fellow workers. His mind was never at rest, and his pencil was connected to his mind by the best conductive tissue I have ever seen in action.

*Is Sex Necessary?* was published in November 1929, enjoying warm reviews and healthy sales (eleven printings totaling 45,000 copies in the first five months). Scott Elledge's biography of White asserts that "eight months earlier the authors had begun to think about collaborating on a parody of some of the works on sex produced by 'heavy writers' (doctors, psychiatrists, and 'other students of misbehavior') with which the market had recently been flooded." Robert Emmet Long's biography of Thurber puts it rather differently: "One day in the late 1920s, Thurber and White discovered that they had each begun parodies of the same subject—the current rash of books that, with pseudoscientific nomenclature, explained sex and psychological adjustment to the layman." In a list of unsuccessful works that Thurber had accumulated by 1927, Long mentions "an elaborate, unpublished parody of current best-sellers, 'Why

We Behave Like Microbe Hunters.' " Certainly Thurber's chapters in *Is Sex Necessary?*—the odd-numbered ones, the glossary, and the preface by "Lt. Col. H. R. L. Le Boutellier, C.I.E."—show the greater enthusiasm for the parodistic premise of the book, that the authors are specialists following in the footsteps of the fictional doctors Karl Zaner and Walter Tithridge, "the deans of American sex." Thurber had a keener interest than White in specifically psychological predicaments; he was, at this tender point in their lives, the more consciously troubled, with his non-starting literary career, his challenged eyesight (he had lost an eye to a brother's arrow in a childhood accident, and the other eye was succumbing to "sympathetic ophthalmia"), and his marriage to Althea née Adams, a tall, ambitious former campus beauty queen at Ohio State University in Columbus. Their union early encountered sexual disarray; Thurber told a friend that "sleeping with Althea is like sleeping with the Statue of Liberty," and she is believed to have inspired the menacing female figure in so many of his drawings.

White's contributions to *Is Sex Necessary?*—the even-numbered chapters, the foreword, "Answers to Hard Questions," and "A Note on the Drawings in This Book"—seem relatively diffident and innocent. Beginning in Chapter II with a bumbling, Benchleyesque embarrassment over distinguishing love from passion, he does work up a certain comedic warmth in Chapter IV concerning *Schmalhausen* trouble, specific to "girls who have taken a small apartment (*schmalhausen*) and are reading the behaviorism essays of Samuel D. Schmalhausen," and ends in Chapter VIII by invoking the minnesingers and the medieval tradition of romantic love, anticipating Denis de Rougemont's epochal *Love in the Western World*. Chapter VIII is the only one jointly composed: Long credits White with "the first and final parts," leaving the hilarious yet heartfelt account of the frigid male's "recessive knee" to Thurber.

Both men had reason for sexual perplexity as 1929 wound down. Thurber felt simultaneously trapped and spurned in his six-year-old marriage to Althea, which had become an erratically "open" one of separate residences and overlooked affairs. A "boxed-in feeling," we read in Chapter VII, can lead to "delusions of persecution [that] may attain astounding proportions." Thurber's inner life, hyperactive since his boyhood, when his natural frailty was intensified by his ophthalmological impairment, could indeed achieve astounding proportions; the convenient diagnosis "nervous breakdown" entered his medical history a number of times, and there were, as he aged, increasingly frequent explosions of wild and rageful drunken behavior. White, at the time of co-authoring *Is Sex Necessary?*, was involved with an older woman, a divorcée with two children, a woman so seductively intelligent and beautifully understanding as to overwhelm the evasive tactics that had kept him a bachelor during his footloose twenties. As a free creative spirit, he had traveled across the country in a model T Ford when the western roads were rudimentary; he had shipped out of the country on a one-way ticket to Alaska. Harold Ross, who keenly wanted him on the editorial bridge of the good ship *New Yorker,* pressed another sort of suit, which White dodged by such maneuvers as taking refuge in a Canadian boys' camp and threatening to become a camp counselor. But Ross and, on the romantic front, Ross's right-hand woman, Katharine Angell, proved too much for the rising writer's vision of an ideal freedom. White and Katharine abruptly married a few days after *Is Sex Necessary?* was published, occasioning this item in Walter Winchell's gossip column:

> News that couldn't wait until Monday: E. B. White, of *The New Yorker*'s comical department and one of the better wits in the town, and Katharine Angell, the managing editor of *The New Yorker,* eloped Tuesday and were sealed up-state.
>
> The groom recently co-authored a book titled (heh-heh) "Is Sex Necessary?"

The wedding was performed in Bedford Village, in a Presbyterian church after the couple failed to find a justice of the peace, and the bride's dog, Daisy (a gift from the Thurbers), got into a fight with the minister's police dog. White later remembered, "It was a very nice wedding— nobody threw anything, and there was a dog fight." The marriage, of which Katharine had told a friend at the time, "If it lasts only a year, it will be worth it," lasted until she died in 1977, and was by all signs a happy and mutually enhancing one.

In *Is Sex Necessary?*, it may have been Thurber who wrote, in the climactic eighth chapter, "Life, as we know, is very insistent; almost daily people become involved with other people," but it was White who observed, in the penultimate paragraph, "An imagined kiss is more easily controlled, more thoroughly enjoyed, and less cluttery than an actual kiss." The danger of entrapment in reality (e.g., women) is a theme common to both writers, both of them nervous, wary men who at this point in their lives could not foresee their future renown or the lasting success of the magazine that had given them professional shelter. Their joint answer to the question the title of their book poses would seem to be, "Maybe, but we'd rather it weren't." Seldom has a book with "sex" in the title had so little good to say for it.

The two men never collaborated on another book, and their office-sharing ended in 1930. Thurber was five years older and yet the more extravagant in his behavior and art. He was a natural show-off, given, like his mother, to amateur theatrics and antic monologues. In his near-blindness he found it entertaining to hoax his friends with uncannily imitated voices over the telephone. Fame held no terrors for him; in 1960, a Broadway revue based on his work, titled *A Thurber Carnival*, was faltering at the box office; he stepped in and played himself, delivering a monologue each night from a chair whisked to the center of the stage on a conveyor belt. Elliott Nugent, his old friend and co-author of the play *The Male Animal*, commented, "That S.O.B. has been trying to get on the stage for forty years, to my certain knowledge." White, in contrast, never spoke in public and appeared onstage only for the mute acceptance of some honorary degrees. Still, as Elledge points out:

> In background and experience the two men had much in common. Their parents had not gone to college. Each had been given as a middle name the name of a Protestant minister. The middle-class culture of Mount Vernon, New York, was not much different from that of Columbus, Ohio. Both had been editors of university newspapers. . . . Both had written scripts for campus musicals. Neither had shown much ability to write fiction; both admired the great American paragraphers.

Both, he could have gone on, became the biological father of one child—Rosemary Thurber, Joel White—and wrote beautiful and, in White's case, classic books for children. Both achieved high literary status without ever publishing a novel for adults. Both were, it is almost unnecessary to say, white, Gentile, Protestant males when to be anything else was to enjoy, in the United States, minority status. In White's chapter "The Sexual Revolution: Being a

Rather Complete Survey of the Entire Sexual Scene," a generic figure called "Man"—of two illustrative drawings by Thurber, one has Thurber's mustache and spectacles and the other White's furrowed brow and central hair-parting—"had come to know enough about permutations and combinations to realize that with millions of Caucasian females to choose from, the chances of his choosing the ideal mate were almost zero." Damsels of African, Asian, or Jewish blood evidently needed not apply. Rereading *Is Sex Necessary?* seventy-five years after its creation, one is more conscious than its good-humored, liberal-minded authors could have been of its phallocratic assumptions and misogynistic tendencies. Thurber, in the chapter "Claustrophobia, or What Every Young Wife Should Know," amusingly relates the case of a husband (born, like Thurber, in 1894) who is heedlessly painted into the bathroom while shaving and then is told by his wife, "You'll simply have to stay in there till the paint dries." He traces, in an increasingly urgent tone, how the difficulties a husband experiences with guest towels and such enigmatic household details lead to "the inception of a Persecution Complex and the slow deterioration of mind and spirit incident upon claustrophobia," and he concludes by decrying the "heavy toll of male minds as the result of the carelessness or stupidity of wives." White ends the next chapter on an equally harsh and abrupt note: "So you see, frigidity in men has many aspects, many angles. To me it is vastly more engrossing than frigidity in women, which is such a simple phenomenon you wonder anybody bothers about it at all." *The Vagina Monologues* lay far in the future.

White and Thurber, though agnostic as adults, were raised as Protestants early in the last century, when the Puritan heritage was still vitally felt in the respectable middle class. Both families were shocked and offended by their sons' chastely racy spoof. White overheard his father say to his mother, "Well, I don't know what *you* think about it, but *I'm* ashamed of it." Thurber's loyal father back in Columbus told an inquirer, "The name sort of bothered me at first. I spent plenty of time dodging the young woman [the librarian] every time I visited the public library." The two writers' voices harmonize in a distrust of sex and resentment of the contortions and submissions that sex exacts from men. The early-twenty-first-century reader, amid the furor over gay marriage and in the wake of the Pill, the free-loving counterculture of the sixties, the women's liberation of the seventies, and the outing of AIDS in the eighties, must make an effort to feel how sweetly daring it was for these two non-Casanovas to put their modest experience and considerable qualms at the service of this spoof, which for all its flimsiness and signs of carefree haste says much that is honest and true about human sexual discomfort.

The drawings, of course, keep the text from ever too

heavily touching the ground. As White explains in his note on the drawings, it was he, in the offices of the young *New Yorker*, who noticed them, retrieved them from the wastebasket, inked them in, and presented them to Harper and Brothers as the finished illustrations. It was a stroke of critical genius on White's part, and it launched Thurber's career as an artist: After *Is Sex Necessary?* appeared, Ross began to run Thurber's cartoons in the magazine, and they became, along with those of Arno and Hokinson and Addams, signature ornaments. After White's marriage, the collaborative fever between the two "Talk" writers cooled, and, as the magazine prospered and expanded, the office the size of a hall bedroom no longer needed to be shared. But the names of Thurber and White were linked for good, and the Whites never quite surrendered their old friendship to Thurber's later provocations and troubled egotism. *Is Sex Necessary?*, breezy and slight and overextended as it is, has never been out of print; it stands as a rare conjunction of singular talents, a fusion bred of close professional quarters. Its jests cast shadows; melancholy and anxiety underlie its high spirits. *Sex isn't everything*, the book seems to say; *but, then, what is?*

# IS SEX NECESSARY?

# INTRODUCTION

THE fall of 1929 is remembered by most people as the time of the stock market crash and the beginning of the great depression. The fall of 1929, however, is memorable to me because of two other events: *Is Sex Necessary?* was published by Harper, and I got married. Walter Winchell, a young columnist of the period, compressed both events into a single newsy sentence, thereby achieving one of the happy juxtapositions that have made him famous. The Winchell notice (and the book itself) gave my parents quite a turn; but the book began to sell, either despite the depression or because of it, and my marriage withstood the inevitable strain of being associated with such a title. Now that twenty-one years have gone roaring over the dam, it is presumably permissible to make a few appropriate remarks about *Is Sex Necessary?*—at any rate, the publisher has asked me to do so.

When Thurber and I concocted the book, we were riding one of the many small waves that, taken all together, created the turbulence of the late 1920's. Those were unstable years. The economy was blown up beyond reasonable dimensions, and nerves were frazzled. The literature of the period blossomed with deep and lugubrious books on sex and marriage. The Freudian concept had been accepted quite generally. Doctors, psychiatrists, and other students of misbehavior were pursuing sex to the last ditch, and the human animal seemed absorbed in self-analysis. I am sure that Dr. Joseph Collins, one of the literary characters of the day, found it more profitable to write *The Doctor Looks at Love and Life* and *The Doctor Looks at Marriage and Medicine* than to sit and look at a sphygmomanometer. The tonsil was clearly bowing to the psyche in 1929.

Thurber and I were neither more, nor less, interested in the subject of love and marriage than anybody else of our age in that era. I recall that we were both profoundly interested in earning a living, and I think we somehow managed, simultaneously, to arrive at the conclusion that (to borrow a phrase from Mr. Wolcott Gibbs) the heavy writers had got sex down and were breaking its arm. We were determined that sex should retain its high spirits. So we decided to spoof the medical books and, incidentally, to have a quick look at love and passion.

As I glance back at 1929 from this distance, I feel sure that there must have been ways we could have been improving our time to better advantage, but whatever they were, we ignored them momentarily. When the two of us walked into Harper's reception room carrying the finished manuscript and a sheaf of Thurber's pencil drawings, we not only didn't give the book twenty years, we didn't give it twenty minutes. Neither of us felt any assurance that it would be accepted for publication. Our interview with Eugene Saxton, who batted for Harper, did not greatly encourage us. We gave him the manuscript and delivered a brief sales talk. Then we spread a few drawings on the floor for him to look at. The American public was at that time not aware of James Thurber's art, and I'm sure Saxton had never seen a Thurber picture. Foreseeing that such unorthodox illustrations might catch a publisher off his guard, I had taken two steps that I thought might improve our chances. I had written an explanatory note about Thurber's pictures and I had bought a bottle of Higgins waterproof ink and inked some of them in, to make them stand out a little clearer. This desecration shocks me today, but it didn't seem out of order at the time. Jim always drew in very light pencil strokes, usually on yellow paper and usually while thinking of something else, and his pictures were so numerous that he and I had both acquired the habit of tossing them into the wastebasket almost as fast as he produced them. They were more a problem of disposal than of anything else. So we just picked a few for the book, and Jim dashed off a few more to fit, and I applied the ink. It took him a few minutes to create them—took me hours to ink them. The difference between genius and pluck.

Mr. Saxton looked at what we had spread out on the

floor and simply said: "These, I take it, are the rough sketches from which the drawings will be produced?"

"No," I said, cheerfully, "these are the drawings themselves."

Then we all three separated in high embarrassment. Harper went ahead and issued the book and now in 1950 it celebrates its twenty-first birthday. As books go it has had a good little life and gives signs of not being through yet. I wish it many happy returns.

I don't know what, if anything, has happened to sex in twenty-one years. I've just reread the book and was amused to find that even in 1929 Thurber had discovered the word "somatic" and thought enough of it to bother to write a footnote about it. This seems, in the light of today, almost uncanny. In some respects *Is Sex Necessary?* is dated; in other respects it is very much abreast of its theme, and has, in fact, the day-after-tomorrow look of those malformed females in the style pictures in Vogue.

During the war, the book was issued in paper-cover form to the Armed Services, and Thurber and I received letters from readers overseas. Some of them asked: "What's all this—we don't get it." Such readers, of course, had been babes in arms in the Schmalhausen era, and were only dimly aware that the book was a parody. But even discounting that, there can be no doubt that the subject of sex and behavior is, to the young today, not the same subject it was to us. There is, I gather, a more relaxed approach to the matter. Passion, to the modern, is not much more mysterious or baffling than a sneeze or a yawn. To the soldier in these later wars, the entire subject of sex can be conveniently reduced to the word "dames." The knowledge we had to acquire through tortuous journeys through medical and psychological books, the young today can acquire in the course of almost any historical novel—or by going to the movies.

I wrote Thurber the other day and asked him please to bring sex up to date for the book. He replied as follows:

"I last had word about Dr. Karl Zaner in 1941 when a correspondent wrote me that she had seen him about town, walking a little unsteadily and given to muttering inaudibly. There is some reason to believe that Dr. Zaner in his late years has become depressed by a lack of the schematic and the presence of too many variables in the study of sex. An ophthalmologist who studies two thousand similar eye ailments can come up with dependable conclusions, but the scientist of sex, completing his investigation of two thousand persons in love, is just about where he was when he started out. Only two facts, I suppose, can be stated in this fluctuant field, without fear of successful contradiction: young women are still faced with the problem of how to tell popularity from promiscuity, and young men are still up against the equally difficult problem of how to have fun without getting married while they are still making only $37.50 a week. The larger aspects of sex become more and more complex at the hands of the psy-chiatrists. As I understand it, and I am probably wrong, bisexuality is on the increase and the psychiatrists are inclined to view this trend as a development, or even flowering, of the individual. Historians, on the other hand, appear to regard it as an evidence of the decline of the species.

"I have heard nothing from or about Dr. Tithridge since he posed for that drawing of mine twenty-one years ago, the one in which he was enormously involved with a potted plant. My only significant piece of personal re-search in the past two decades had to do with a young lover who asked his sweetheart if she would mind having babies, to which she replied, after a moment's thought, 'I think I could probably stand a very small one.' If there are conclusions to be drawn from this, draw them."

For me this book contains two things that make it all seem worth while: it contains a few of the finest of the early Thurber drawings, and it contains the chapter (writ-ten by Thurber) on "The Nature of the American Male." This chapter, although less popular with readers than some, is, now in 1950, just as sharp and good as it ever was. Since I didn't write it I don't have to pull my praises. As a picture of an age, and an affectionate study of love-kept-under, I believe it is unique and probably indestructible. Taken with the drawings of the sex substitutes of the Übertragung Period, there just isn't anything like it in

American humor. Woman, in the intervening years, has slipped (or jumped) from the pedestal on which the male had placed her. She has taken her seat alongside Man on the bar stool and in the forum. She is doing, you might say, what comes naturally. Whether she was better off before —and whether Man was—Thurber and I shall leave to the young to decide.

E.B.W.

*15 January 1950*

# FOREWORD

DURING the past year, two factors in our civilization have been greatly overemphasized. One is aviation, the other is sex. Looked at calmly, neither diversion is entitled to the space it has been accorded. Each has been deliberately promoted.

In the case of aviation, persons interested in the sport saw that the problem was to simplify it and make it seem safer. They introduced stabilizers and emergency landing fields. Even so, the plain fact remained that very few people were fitted for flying.

With sex, the opposite was true. Everybody was fitted for it, but there was a lack of general interest. The problem in this case was to make sex seem more complex and dangerous. This task was taken up by sociologists, analysts, gynecologists, psychologists, and authors; they approached it with a good deal of scientific knowledge and an immense zeal. They joined forces and made the whole matter of sex complicated beyond the wildest dreams of our fathers. The country became flooded with books. Sex, which had hitherto been a physical expression, became largely mental. The whole order of things changed. To prepare for marriage, young girls no longer assembled a hope chest—they read books on abnormal psychology. If they finally did marry, they found themselves with a large number of sex books on hand, but almost no pretty underwear. Most of them, luckily, never married at all—just continued to read.

It was because we observed how things were going with marriage and love that we set out, ourselves, to prepare a sex book of a different kind. In this venture we were greatly encouraged by our many friends of both sexes, most of whom never thought we could do it. Our method was the opposite of that used by other writers on sex: we saw clearly in what respect they failed, and we profited by their example. We saw, chiefly, that these writers expended their entire emotional energy in their writing and never had time for anything else. The great length of their books (some of them ran into two volumes and came in a cardboard box) testified to their absorption with the sheer business of writing. *They clearly hadn't been out much.* They had been home writing; and meanwhile what was sex doing? Not standing still, you can better believe. So we determined that our procedure would be to approach sex bravely, and frequently. "Approach the subject in a lively spirit," we told ourselves, "and the writing will take care of itself." (It is only fair to say that the writing *didn't* take care of itself; the writing was a lot of work and gave us the usual pain in the neck while we were doing it.)

At any rate we gathered about us a host of congenial people of all types, mostly girls. Gay, somber, petulant, all kinds. We also got a lot of dogs, mostly Scotch terriers, a breed noted for stoicism, bravery, and humor. Thus equipped, we set about the work with a good spirit, and by dint of a rather unusual energy were able to prepare the book for publication and see it through the press without giving up any social engagements or isolating ourselves from the sexual world. Furthermore, all the time we were writing the book, we continued to earn our living—in itself no easy matter.

We early resolved to keep alive our curiosity about things. Wherever we went we asked questions. Aware of the tangled sexual thread running through the pattern of people's lives, we continually asked the question: "Why is it that you never got straightened out?" The answers we got to this question helped us immeasurably.

Although most of our research was in life's laboratory, so to speak, we wish also to express our indebtedness to those authors whose writings on the subject inspired us. How can we forget, in this connection, such men as Will Durant, Samuel D. Schmalhausen, Dr. Joseph Collins, Joseph Wood Krutch, and Gardner Murphy?

Most particularly are we desirous of acknowledging a

debt to those two remarkable men, who, more than any others, gave us the courage to go on; two men without whose example we never could have found in sex a daily inspiration; those two geniuses whom it is our pleasure to call the "deans of American sex,"—Walter Tithridge and Karl Zaner.

# PREFACE

MEN and women have always sought, by one means and another, to be together rather than apart. At first they were together by the simple expedient of being unicellular, and there was no conflict. Later the cell separated, or began living apart, for reasons which are not clear even today, although there is considerable talk. Almost immediately the two halves of the original cell began experiencing a desire to unite again—usually with a half of some other cell. This urge has survived down to our time. Its commonest manifestations are marriage, divorce, neuroses, and, a little less frequently, gun-fire.

When society decided it would have to set up laws to govern these polymorphous manifestations of a once simple urge which had got out of hand, it did so without a very clear notion of sex as we know it today. It did not realize that direction of the Love Urge by outside forces of law and order must be subversive of the complete flowering of the individual—and is there anything in life more wonderful than a completely flowered individual, man or woman?

Yet under all the weight of social regulation, the ancient desire to unite and to separate and to unite again, usually with some one else, has survived, for the simple reason that it is stronger than man-made law and because cells, as now constituted, are more astute than the police. They have to be. Thus we find men and women being consistently together even against the rigorous dictates of a prescribed behaviorism to whose institutional coldness the warmth of their emotional natures is irrevocably opposed. And so on.

As far as I can make out, the authors of this remarkable book subscribe to the modern ideal of freedom in sex, but do not believe that marriage has yet been proved a failure in every case, nor that sex can profitably be examined entirely apart from that old institution. In this viewpoint the authors and myself are at one, which is probably the reason I was asked to write an introduction.

Marriage, as an instrument, is a well-nigh perfect thing. The trouble is that it cannot be successfully applied to the present-day emotional relationships of men and women. It could much more easily be applied to something else, possibly professional tennis. As they now stand, marriage and sex militate against each other. If marriage is to be retained it must be perfected to meet the new demands and intricacies of sex. There is, doubtless, a discoverable plane on which marriage and sex, the institutional and the emotional, could meet and, as who should say, become friends. Not only marriage, however, but sex as well, would have to make certain concessions. Tempered by this balanced viewpoint, one must find it, then, logically impossible to pose only the question. "What is wrong with marriage?" It becomes necessary also to pose the question, "What is wrong with sex?" For if it is plausible to assume

*Early Woman.*

that something may be so radically wrong with a well-nigh perfect institutional device that it might be well for society to abandon it, one must, in all fairness, entertain the suspicion that something may be so wrong with a well-nigh perfect emotional relationship that it might be well for society to abandon it, too.

People never have been satisfied with marriage. If the contracting parties are satisfied with it, some one else isn't. How often one hears the expression, "I don't know what she sees in him." As a matter of fact, however, we hear that expression less frequently today than we used to, because psychology has enabled us to know what she does see in him. There is, however, still considerable doubt as to what he sees in her. Some authorities claim that no man can see all there is to see in a woman, because she is too complicated and mysterious for him. This notion—that Woman is more incomprehensible than Man—has persisted for centuries. It is of a piece with the legend that Woman is deserving of a certain form of idolatrous worship, a legend that grew up in the early ages of the world. When Man first came into being, he did not think that the female was extraordinary. He did not think that anything was extraordinary. The world was unattractive physically, and a little dull. There was no vegetation, and without vegetation there can be no fancy. Then trees came into existence. It was trees that first made Man begin to brood. In pondering their leafy intricacies he got his first crude concept of beauty. He used to tear great branches out of trees and take them home to his cave woman. "Here," he would say to her, "lie on these." The man then reclined in a corner of the cave and watched the woman's hair mingle with the leaves, and her eyes shine through them, until he fell asleep. His dreams were troubled. Woman came into his dreams as a tree, then a tree came into his dreams as a woman. He also got her eyes, shining through the leaves, all mixed up with the moon. Out of this curious and lamentable confusion grew the tendency in Man's mind to identify Woman with the phenomena of the burgeoning earth and the mysteries of the illimitable heavens. As time went on Man rather enjoyed cultivating this idea. It was something to think about. It wasn't much, but it was something. Thus was the subconscious born, with all its strange mixture of fact and symbol.

As the vegetation of the earth grew more luxuriant Man grew more moody. Each new plant represented something

*Early Conference.*

that he could not easily fit into his practicable scheme of things (the tomato, for example, wasn't fitted in until late in the nineteenth century). For the first wild iris, Man saw no conceivable use. However, he plucked it. It had, he noticed, that curious color, or pigmentation, which he associated with only two other things—the sky and Woman's eyes. He brooded upon this astounding coincidence overlong. Often he got wet through, standing in a bog, contemplating a blue flag. Then he would take it home and give it to his mate.

All these things operated to bring about in Man's mind an inclination to identify the wonders of the earth and sky with the physical fact of his mate's existence. He decided they must have a great deal in common, these wonders and this woman. What that was he determined to find out. Too proud at first, too male, to take his mate into his confidence in the matter of his uncertainties, he got to tramping the bogs and woods at night, seeking the answer. He bayed questions at the moon, he beseeched the trees to speak, he shouted at the wild iris. There was no answer. It was then that it occurred to Man that, since these things could not tell him the answer to the riddle of the universe, the only possible source of that information must repose in the living creature which he identified with them, the woman with skyey eyes and leafy hair. Then came that important night when one of the early men resolutely rose from his knees, under the moon, and started back to his cave to demand from his mate an explanation of all these mysteries. On the way a star fell. Those ages were notable for falling meteors. This one frightened the man as it crashed sizzling through the trees and buried itself with a moan in the ground. He ran the rest of the way home, arriving breathless and white.

"Wha' was 'at?" he croaked, pointing behind him. His mate saw nothing but the waving of fern fronds in the wind, the form of some animal slinking into the woods.

"It is nothing," she said, and smiled, and ran her hand through his hair.

Right then and there Man conceived the notion that

Woman was so closely associated, so inextricably entwined with the wonders and terrors of the world, that she had no fear of them. She was in quiet league with the forces of life. She was an integral part of the stars and the moon, she was one with the trees and the iris in the bog. He fell down on his knees, the pitiable idiot, and grasped her about the waist.

It is inconceivable that a myth as strong as this belief in the ineffability of Woman, as deeply rooted in the soils of time, can ever be completely eradicated. However fantastical, however untrue, crotchet or whim, fancy or foible, there it is and there it has always been. To destroy it would be to put the female properly in her place, as a plain, unadorned unit in the senseless but unending pattern of biological continuity. Romantic love would disappear. Life would be simplified. Neuroses would vanish. But Man clings to his ancient and silly value. What it has done to him is quite easy to see. It has subordinated him to Woman, for one thing. The emotional nature of the male has either been overlooked altogether or greatly disparaged. "Isn't that just like a man?" is an all-too-glib and common expression. It implies that one can virtually ascribe to all men the simple reactions which, in a number of men, inexpertly observed, have proved *likely* to take place. (The italic is mine.)

Observers have been too prone to hold that the male is negligible, and to overemphasize the importance of the female. Thus we find such keen analysts as Ira S. Wile and Mary Day Winn[1] asserting that "anyone who wishes to understand modern marriage must center his attention on woman and find out what she thinks of it and what she intends to do about it." This is the old Bridegroom Fallacy —the notion, to paraphrase Miss Loos, that the bride is divine but that the bridegroom is just nothing. Unless more stress is laid, and pretty quickly, too, upon the complexity of the male, and the importance of what he is thinking about and what he intends to do, or at least what he would like to do, we are never going to arrive at a norm. How often do you hear it said that the little whims and desires of a man should be cherished, or even listened to? You don't hear it said at all. What you do hear is that "the way to a man's heart is through his stomach." A thing like that hardens a man. He may eat his spinach and say nothing, but he is being hardened just the same.

The American male, because of the remarkable stress laid upon woman in this country, has been understood least of all males. There has been no completely successful attempt to state his case until the authors of this extraordinary book came along. I do not know who they are. In places they do not seem to be themselves. But they've got something. (A lot of what they have they seem to have got from Zaner and Tithridge, which is all right with me.) At any rate, they state the case for the American man clear-

---

[1] *Marriage in the Modern Manner.*

ly and plausibly. At the same time they have by no means neglected the female. It takes two to make a neurosis, and nobody knows that any better than White and Thurber, unless it's Zaner and Tithridge.

Herein are examined, therefore, both men and women, male and female, Man and Woman—not only in themselves, but in their curious reactions to each other. The term "reaction" seems to be used in this book to include not only those quick, unpremeditated reflexes which cause so much trouble, but also those slowly formulated prejudices, doubts, and suspicions which cause even more trouble. If this book does anything at all toward straightening out the lamentable mess that things have got into in America—and I certainly think it will—the authors will feel amply repaid for their pains, which consisted in large part, they tell me, of insults.

Lt. Col. H. R. L. Le Boutellier, C.I.E.
Schlaugenschloss Haus,
King's Byway,
Boissy-le-Doux sur Seine.
July 15, 1929

# CHAPTER I

# The Nature of the American Male: A Study of Pedestalism

IN NO other civilized nation are the biological aspects of love so distorted and transcended by emphasis upon its sacredness as they are in the United States of America. In China it's all biology. In France it's a mixture of biology and humor. In America it's half, or two-thirds, psyche. The Frenchman's idea, by and large, is to get the woman interested in him as a male. The American idea is to point out, first of all, the great and beautiful part which the stars, and the infinite generally, play in Man's relationship to women. The French, Dutch, Brazilians, Danes, etc., can proceed in their amours on a basis entirely divorced from the psyche. The Chinese give it no thought at all, and never have given it any thought. The American would be lost without the psyche, lost and a little scared.

As a result of all this there is more confusion about love in America than in all the other countries put together. As soon as one gets the psychical mixed up with the physical—a thing which is likely to happen quite easily in a composing-room, but which should not happen anywhere else at all—one is almost certain to get appetite mixed up with worship. This is a whole lot like trying to play golf with a basketball, and is bound to lead to maladjustments.

The phenomenon of the American male's worship of the female, which is not so pronounced now as it was, but is still pretty pronounced, is of fairly recent origin. It developed, in fact, or reached its apex, anyway, in the early years of the present century. There was nothing like it in the preceding century. Throughout the nineteenth century the American man's amatory instincts had been essentially economic. Marriage was basically a patriotic concern, the idea being to have children for the sake of the commonwealth. This was bad enough, but nevertheless it is far less dangerous to get the commonwealth mixed up with love than to get the infinite mixed up with love.

There was not a single case of nervous breakdown, or neurosis, arising from amatory troubles, in the whole cycle from 1800 to 1900, barring a slight flare-up just before the Mexican and Civil wars. This was because love and marriage and children stood for progress, and progress is—or was—a calm, routine business. "Mrs. Hopkins," a man would say to the lady of his choice (she was a widow in this case)—"Mrs. Hopkins, I am thinking, now that George[1] has been dead a year, you and I should get married and have offspring. They are about to build the Union Pacific,

---

[1] The late George Hopkins.

you know, and they will need men." Because parents can't always have men-children when they want them, this led to almost as many women as men working on the Union Pacific, which in turn led to the greater stature of women in the present Northwest than in any other part of the nation. But that is somewhat beside the point. The point is that men and women, husbands and wives, suitors and sweethearts, in the last century lived without much sentiment and without any psycho-physical confusion at all. They missed a certain amount of fun, but they avoided an even greater amount of pother (see Glossary). They did not worry each other with emotional didoes. There was no hint of Pleasure-Principle. Everything was empiric, almost somatic.[1]

This direct evasion of the Love Urge on the part of Americans of the last century was the nuclear complex of the psycho-neurosis as we know it today, and the basis for that remarkable reaction against patriotic sex which was to follow so soon after the Spanish-American war.

At the turn of the century, the nation was on a sound

---

[1] The word "somatic" has been left out of the glossary because of the confusion which the dictionary itself seems to be in over the meaning of the term. "Pertaining to the wall of the body" is as close as the New International comes to what we have in mind here, but it goes right on to use "parietal" as a synonym and parietal means "pertaining to order within the buildings of a college." Then again the word goes back to the old Indian, or East Indian, root *Soma* which means a god, a liquor, and an asclepiadaceous climbing shrub (*Sarcostemma acidum*). Furthermore, if your eyes stray even a fraction of an inch, in looking up "somatic," you are in "sölvsbergite" which includes the feldspars, ægirite, grorudite, and tinguaite.

economic basis and men had the opportunity to direct their attention away from the mechanics of life to the pleasures of living. No race can leap lightly, however, from an economic value to an emotional value. There must be a long period of *Übertragung*, long and tedious. Men were not aware of this, thirty years ago, because the science of

Fig. 1.
*Sex Substitutes (Übertragung Period): Baseball.*

psychology was not far advanced, but nature came to their aid by supplying a temporary substitute for an emotional sex life, to tide them over during the period of *Übertragung*. This substitute took the form of games. Baseball assumed a new and enormous importance, prize-fighting reached its heyday; horse-racing became an absorption, bicycling a craze.

Now women, naturally intraverts, could not easily identify themselves with baseball or prize-fighting (they admired Christy Mathewson and Terry McGovern, but that was about all); they took but slowly to horse-racing; and they giggled and acted the fool when they first tried to balance themselves on a bicycle. They drew away from

Fig. 2.
*Sex Substitutes (Übertragung Period): Bowling.*

men and from men's concerns, therefore—there was no more of the old Union Pacific camaraderie—and began to surround the mere fact of their biological destiny with a nimbus of ineffability. It got so that in speaking of birth and other natural phenomena, women seemed often to be discussing something else, such as the Sistine Madonna or the aurora borealis. They became mysterious to themselves and to men; they became suddenly, in their own eyes, as capable of miracle and as worthy of worship as Juno and her sisters. This could not go on. The conflict was ineluctable.

When men, wearied of games, turned to women with that urgency so notable in the American male for its simplicity and directness, they found them unprepared for acceptance and surrender. The process of adjustment in courtship and in marriage became more involved than it had ever been before in the history of the country, if not in the history of the world. The new outdoors type of American man, with all his strength and impetuosity, was not easily to be put off. But the female, equipped with a Defense far superior in polymorphous ingenuities to the rather simple Attack of the male, was prepared. She developed and perfected the Diversion Subterfuge. Its purpose was to put Man in his place. Its first manifestation was fudge-making.

The effectiveness of fudge-making in fending off the male and impressing him with the female's divine unapproachability can not be over-estimated. Neither can its potentiality as a nuclear complex. The flitting from table to stove, the constant necessity of stirring the boiling confection, the running out-of-doors to see if the candy had cooled and hardened, served to abort any objective demonstrations at all on the part of the male. He met this situation with a strong Masculine Protest. He began to bring

## FUDGE-MAKING

"The female, equipped with a Defense far superior in polymorphous ingenuities to the rather simple Attack of the male, developed, and perfected, the Diversion Subterfuge. The first manifestation of this remarkable phenomenon was fudge-making."

a box of candy with him when he called, so that there would not be any more fudge-making. These years constituted the great Lowney's era in this country. Brought back to where she had started, face to face with the male's simple desire to sit down and hold her, the female, still intent upon avoidance of the tactual, retaliated by suggesting Indoor Pastimes—one of the greatest of all Delay Mechanisms. All manner of parlor games came into being at this period, notably charades,[1] which called for the presence of other persons in the room (Numerical Protection). The American male's repugnance to charades, which is equaled, perhaps, by his repugnance to nothing else at all, goes back to those years. The Masculine Protest, in this case, was a counter-suggestion of some games of his own, in which there was a greater possibility of personal contact. His first suggestions were quite primitive, such as that it would be fun to count up to a hundred by kissing. The female's response was the famous one of Osculatory Justification. There must be, she decreed, more elaborate reasons for kissing than a mere exhibition of purposeless arithmetical virtuosity. Thus Post Office and Pillow were finally devised, as a sort of compromise. Neither was satisfactory to either sex. The situation became considerably strained and relationships finally trailed off into the even less satisfactory expedient of going for long rides on a tandem bicycle, which has had its serious effects upon the

[1] See Glossary, definition No. (1).

nature of the American man. He liked, for one thing, to do tricks on a bicycle. The contraption was new to him, and he wanted to do tricks on it. One trick that he liked especially was riding backwards. But there wasn't one woman in ten thousand, riding frontwards on the rear seat of a tandem wheel, who would permit her consort to ride backwards on the front seat. The result of all this was not adjustment, but irritability. Man became frustrated.

Frustration wrought its inevitable results. Men began to act jumpy and strange. They were getting nowhere at all with women. The female gradually assumed, in men's eyes, as she had in her own, the proportions of an unattainable deity, something too precious to be touched. The seed of Pedestalism was sown. The male, in a sort of divine discontent, began to draw apart by himself. This produced that separation of the physical and the psychic which causes the adult to remain in a state of suspended love, as if he were holding a bowl of goldfish and had nowhere to put it. This condition nowadays would lead directly to a neurosis, but in those days men were unable to develop a neurosis because they didn't know how. Men withdrew, therefore, quietly and morosely, to their "dens." It was the epoch of the den in America. Some marvelous ones sprang into being. Their contents were curiously significant. Deprived of possessing the female, the male worked off his Possessive Complex by collecting all manner of bibelots and bric-à-brac. The average den contained a paper-weight

"There wasn't one woman in ten thousand, riding frontwards on the rear seat of a tandem wheel, who would permit her consort to ride backwards on the front seat. The result of all this was not adjustment, but irritability. Man became frustrated."

from Lookout Mountain, a jagged shell from Chickamauga, a piece of wood from the *Maine*, pictures of baseball players with beards, pictures of bicycle champions, a yellowing full-page photograph of Admiral Schley, a letter-opener from Niagara Falls, a lithograph of Bob Fitzsim-

*Fig. 3.*
*Sex Substitutes (Übertragung Period): Craps.*

mons, a musket-badge from the G. A. R. parade, a red tumbler from the state fair, a photograph of Julia Marlowe, a monk's head match-holder, a Malay kriss, five pipe racks, a shark's tooth, a starfish, a snapshot of the owner's father's bowling team, colored pictures of Natural Bridge and Balanced Rock, a leather table runner with an Indian chief on it, and the spangled jacket of a masquerade costume, softly shedding its sequins.

The den was the beginning of male sublimation in this country, but the fruits of that sublimation were slow in ripening. At the start, in fact, they were in a state of absolute suspension. Man began to preoccupy himself with

*Fig. 4.*
*Sex Substitutes (Übertragung Period): Six-day Bicycle Racing.*

anything, no matter how trivial, which might help him to "forget," as the lay expression has it. He thought up childish diversions, at which one person can amuse himself, and to justify his absorption in these futile pastimes he exaggerated their importance, as we shall see. These diversions included the diabolo, the jig-saw puzzle, linked nails and linked keys, which men took apart and put back together again, and most important of all, pigs-in-clover.

During this period almost no achievements of value, in art, science, or engineering, were forthcoming in the nation. Art, indeed, consisted chiefly of putting strange devices on boxes with the aid of a wood-burning set. The commonest device was the swastika, whose curiously distorted conformation bears no discernible relationship to any known phallic symbolism. Those years were blank, idle, lost years. Outside affairs of all kinds were neglected. Men retired to their dens and were not seen for days. The panic of 1907 was a direct result. It might be interesting to examine into a typical case history of the period.

### CASE HISTORY

George Smith, aged 32, real estate operator. Unmarried, lived with mother. No precocious mother fixation. Had freed his libido without difficulty from familial objects, and was eager to marry. Had formed an attachment in 1899, at the age of 29, with a young virgin. Her Protective Reactions had been immediate and lasted over a period of three years, during which he had never even held her hand. Defense Devices: usually euchre(four-handed), or pedro. Definite and frequent fudge-making subterfuge. Post Office and Pillow, both with low degree of success.

Smith's separation between the physical and the psychic occurred in 1902, the direct stimuli presenting themselves on June 6th of that year, examination (by Dr. Matthiessen) showed. On that day Smith ran, frightened, from a barbershop in Indianapolis, where he lived. Inside the shop, on the floor, a middle-aged man named Herschel Queeper had thrown a fit. Queeper had been trying for two days to get three little balls, under a glass in a tiny round box, to roll into an opening made for them (common pigs-in-clover puzzle). But no sooner would he get the third one in than one, or perhaps both, of the others would roll out. Mrs. Queeper was beginning to wonder where he was.

Smith withdrew to his den and pondered and fiddled around and made Unconscious Drawings (Cf. Plates I, II, III and IV). He turned his attention from the object of his amorous affections to a consideration of the problems of pigs-in-clover. The usual Justification of Occupation occurred. It took the form of exaggerating the importance of finding out whether the puzzle could possibly be solved, and of working out a methodology of solving it more readily, if it could be solved at all. The case procured one of the little boxes and began to roll the balls toward the opening. At first he set about it quite calmly. There were no immediate signs of mental deterioration, either malignant or benign. But although the case got all the balls into the opening, thus proving that it could be done, he never got them all in at the same time. In the second month he threw a brief fit. This, today, would ordinarily prove the first step toward a complete physico-psychic breakdown, but in those days neuroses were staved

### UNCONSCIOUS DRAWING: PLATE I.

Unconscious drawings, as they are called in psychoanalytical terminology, are made by people when their minds are a blank. This drawing was made by Floyd Neumann, of South Norwalk. It represents the Male Ego being importuned by, but refusing to yield to, Connecticut Beautiful.

off longer, owing to the general ignorance of psychology, and Smith not only calmly examined the effect of the fit upon himself, without calling in any scientists, but determined to go on and examine the effect of fits upon others. He decided, however, that it would be difficult to examine the effects of puzzle-fits upon men, because men brooked

*"Furthermore, the animal was profoundly incurious about the puzzle."*

no examination when they were intent upon puzzles, and so he hit on the idea of having his dog, an animal named Dewey, play with the little round box until it threw a fit. But when he called in his dog he found, after several experiments, that the dog could not hold the box in either its right or left paw.[1] Furthermore, the animal was profoundly incurious about the puzzle.[2]

Undismayed, Smith decided that somewhere in Indianapolis there must be a dog adroit enough to handle the box

[1] This presented a difficulty that has not been overcome to this day.
[2] This disinterest held good up until the day of the dog's death.

and sagacious enough to grasp the idea behind it, and with a view to finding such an animal, he determined to get all the dogs in town, and all the pigs-in-clover puzzles in town, into one room and see what would happen. (Apotheosis Complex, with Plurality Fallacy.)

Smith was able, however, to round up only about 85 per cent of the dogs of the city, because there were many who were too busy to get away at the time. Even so, 85 per cent of the dogs in Indianapolis was more than had ever been got together in one room before. The case attempted to explain the problem to the dogs in short, one-syllable talks, but the bedlam was too loud and too prolonged for him to make himself heard. Fifty or more St. Bernards and a few dozen Chesapeake spaniels listened, half-heartedly, but the others made holiday. Furthermore, eighty-four bulldogs would not permit themselves to be muzzled, and this added to Smith's difficulties. Thus, on the fifth day of the singular experiment, Smith, hearing a remarkable hullaballoo belowstairs (he worked in the attic), descended to the parlor, where he discovered the bulldogs engaged in a sort of tug-of-war, using a body Brussels carpet as a rope. (The case's mother had several days before retreated to French Lick, in a rundown condition.)

Smith grasped the carpet firmly, with some idea of wresting it away from the dogs, whereupon all of them save three began to pull against him.[1] The Exaggeration

---

[1] These three had closed their eyes, to hang on, and did not see Smith.

**UNCONSCIOUS DRAWING: PLATE II.**
This was drawn by Peter Zinsner, 564 DeKalb Avenue, Brooklyn, without knowing it. We here see Sublimation in conflict with the Libido. Peter has reached a point in life where women seem so divine he doesn't dare call them up on the phone. Yet they still call him.

Complex under which the case was laboring gave him strength enough to meet with some small success in his first efforts to take the carpet away from the dogs. He pulled them as far as the bay window in the parlor, largely because they had not settled down seriously to winning. When they did, however, the total of three hundred and twenty-four solidly implanted feet and the virtually immeasurable tugging potentiality were too much for Smith. He was slowly pulled out into the hall, through the front door, and into the street. He stubbornly contested every inch of the way until a drug store, three blocks away, was reached. Here some one had the presence of mind to call out the fire department.

Dr. Matthiessen, who took the case at about this period in its development, attempted to reduce the Magnification of Objective, first by Analytic Reasoning, and then by cold applications. Neither was successful. Matthiessen could not divert the libido. Smith declined to resume his interest in the feminine object of his affections, and insisted that his experiment with puzzles was a glorious project for the benefit of mankind.

It was sheer accident that saved the patient—not Dr. Matthiessen. Smith finally refused Dr. Matthiessen admittance to his house, nor would he go to the doctor's office, claiming that he did not believe in psychology, but one day he dropped one of the little pigs-in-clover puzzles and broke the glass in it. He then found that he did not have to roll the balls into the openings, *but could push them in with his finger.* He got a hammer and broke the glass in all the thousands of puzzles he had brought to his home for the dogs, and solved every one of the puzzles by pushing, not rolling. This instantly released him from his complex by the Gordian Knot principle of complex release. He thus gained the necessary confidence and sense of power to feel worthy of the woman with whom he was in love, and he finally married her. The marriage was of average success.

Marriages, however, were frequently delayed much longer than in the case of George Smith, and it was not, indeed, until 1909 that the usual norm was restored. Meanwhile, in between the time of the first general separation of the physical and the psychic in this country, and the final culmination in marriages, a period of sublimation set in. This followed directly on the heels of the remarkable and lamentable era of preoccupation with trivial diversions and was characterized by an extravert interest in truly important projects and activities. The airplane was brought to a high stage of development, the telephone transmitter was perfected, tungsten replaced carbon as a filament for incandescent lamps, better books were written, art progressed, there was a cultural advance generally and the birth of a new Æsthetic, and people began to get at the

This drawing was made from an old 1901 lantern slide often used by Dr. Karl Zaner in his illustrated lecture, "What Can We Learn from Animals?" Dr. Zaner has always contended that we can learn nothing of importance from animals beyond a few pointers on the art of relaxation. "Their general activities are, as a rule, not only meaningless to man, but frequently to themselves as well. This particular cat, for example, probably had nothing special in mind at all."

real facts in the Thaw case. Nevertheless, Pedestalism has left its serious effects. It is doubtful if they will fully wear off for another fifty or seventy-five years.

# CHAPTER II

# How to Tell Love from Passion

AT A certain point in every person's amours, the question arises: "Am I in love, or am I merely inflamed by passion?"

It is a disturbing question. Usually it arises at some inopportune moment: at the start of a letter, in the middle of an embrace, at the end of a day in the country. If the person could supply a direct, simple, positive answer—if he could say convincingly, "I am in love," or, "This is not love, this is passion"—he would spare himself many hours of mental discomfort. Almost nobody can arrive at so simple a reply. The conclusion a man commonly arrives at, after tossing the argument about, is something after this fashion: "I am in love, all right, but just the same I don't like the way I looked at Miriam last night." Or, "Mirabel is a tidy little wench, and in that case why do I waste time composing a quatrain for her, to be sent with a crushed spray of lilac? Why don't I just go right over?"

One reason a man has trouble telling love from passion is because neither term has been clearly defined. Even after one has experienced love, one finds difficulty defining it. Likewise, one may define it and then have all kinds of trouble experiencing it, because, once having defined it, one is in too pompous a frame of mind ever again to submit to its sweet illusion. By and large, love is easier to experience before it has been explained—easier and cleaner.

*"At a certain point in every person's amours, the question arises: 'Am I in love, or am I merely inflamed by passion?'"*

The same holds true of passion. Understanding the principles of passion is like knowing how to drive a car; once mastered, all is smoothed out; no more does one experience the feeling of perilous adventure, the misgivings, the diverting little hesitancies, the wrong turns, the false starts, the glorious insecurity. All is smoothed out, and all, so to speak, is lost.

The word "love" is used loosely by writers, and they know it. Furthermore, the word "love" is accepted loosely by readers, and *they* know it. There are many kinds of love, but for the purposes of this article I shall confine my discussion to the usual hazy interpretation: the strange bewilderment which overtakes one person on account of another person. Thus, when I say love in this article, you will take it to mean *the pleasant confusion which we know exists*. When I say passion, I *mean* passion.

I have mentioned that the question of deciding whether a feeling be love or passion arises at inopportune moments, such as at the start of a letter. Let us say you have sat down to write a letter to your lady. There has been a normal amount of preparation for the ordeal, such as clearing a space on the desk (in doing which you have become momentarily interested in a little article in last month's *Scribner's* called, "Plumbing the Savage," and have stood for a minute reading the first page and deciding to let it go), and the normal amount of false alarms, such as sitting down and discovering that you have no cigarettes. (Note: if you think you can write the letter without cigarettes, it is not love, it is passion.) Finally you get settled and you write the words; "Anne darling." If you like commas, you put a comma after "darling"; if you like colons, a colon; if dashes, a dash. If you don't care *what* punctuation mark you put after "darling," the chances are you are in love—although you may just be uneducated, who knows?

**UNCONSCIOUS DRAWING: PLATE III.**
This is the work of Grace McFadden, aged 11, of Bucyrus, Ohio (R. F. D. #3, Bucyrus 6021, Ring 3), and was drawn on the day that Principal K. L. Mooney, of the Paulding County Concentration Grade Schools, was married. Here the Pleasure-Principle and the Wish Motive are both over-shadowed by the Bridegroom Fallacy.

Now, you have written the words "Anne darling" and have put a punctuation mark there. You pause for just a second, and in that second you are lost. "Darling?" you say to yourself. "Darling? Is she my darling, or isn't she? And if she *is* my darling, as I have so brazenly set down on this sheet of paper, what caused me to take such a long, critical look at the girl in the red-and-brown scarf this morning when I was breakfasting in the Brevoort? If I can be all aglow about a girl in a red-and-brown scarf in the early morning, is Anne my darling, or am I just kidding myself?"

Then follows a brief estimate of the comparative beauty of Anne and the girl in the scarf, with the girl in the scarf coming out half a length ahead. This is followed by a short dialogue which you hold with yourself.

"What if she *was* prettier?" you say. "What does that amount to? I'm not a child. I know there's more to the story than mere physical beauty."

"What more is there?" you quietly demand, testing yourself out.

"Oh, there's quality of mind, and community of interest, and chemical attraction [chemical attraction is a term you've picked up recently from reading books on sex and life]. When I get right down to it, if I were to meet that girl in the scarf, I probably wouldn't like her."

"No, but you want to meet her, all the same, don't you?"

"Well . . . I mean . . . a man can't; I mean . . ."

"Yah, you know you want to meet her!"

"Aw, shut up!"

Having got nowhere with that theme, you again bend to the mighty task of writing the first sentence of the letter. A minute or two of quiet brooding and the truth comes to you that you have nothing to say, that you wrote all the news yesterday, that you consider it pretty silly to be writing another letter so soon, and that if anyone were to ask you, you don't really want to write Anne a letter at all.

"Well, so that's the way the wind blows!" you say to yourself, contemptuously. "So *that's* the way things are between Anne and you! Not wanting to write her. So it's come to that. Well, it's about time you got wise to yourself. If you don't love Anne it's certainly high time you found it out, in justice to both Anne and yourself. In other words, you never loved Anne at all—you merely gave in to an infatuation. You were thinking about the physical side of the affair; yes, sir, you *desired* Anne, that's what you did. You *desired* her! Why, you dirty, low-down, two-faced old voluptuary you . . ."

The utter shame of this situation breaks your spirit and you lay down your pen, light up a cigarette, and pace up and down the room. Suddenly you dash to the desk, with a look of woeful determination, seize the pen, and write (after the words "Anne darling," which are good and dry by this time): "I have been wanting to tell you something

**AMERICAN MALE POSTURES: PLATE I.**

American men, more than any others, permit the complexities of the psycho-physical world to get them down. Often, while down, they will pass each other going somewhere, and exchange a small greeting.

for a long time. We must look things straight in the face, Anne." You then look things straight in the face for ten minutes, during which you don't write a word, and end by tearing the letter up and quickly dashing off another, which reads: "Anne, I'm awfully tired tonight, nervous, etc., and if I wrote you it would just be a bunch of hooey, so think I will wait till tomorrow before writing. Love, Bert." This you mail at the corner and spend the rest of the evening trying to read "Plumbing the Savage," which results finally in sleep—sleep troubled by dreams of savages wearing loin cloths of a familiar red-and-brown material.

This vexing disbelief in one's own illusion of love is experienced most alarmingly by persons of literary inclinations. Yet with them the reaction comes in quite the opposite manner. Writing is a form of sexual expression (Zaner goes further: he says writing *is* sex), and it takes just as much out of a person. Thus, a person with a bent for creative literature approaches the task of writing a love letter with an excitation of the spirit surpassing anything in the realm of pure eroticism. He anticipates it for hours, mulling over in his mind the possible material, enlarging on anecdotes, rounding off pledges of affection, sharpening similes, sharpening pencils; he comes to the writing of it with immense zeal and a rather nice control of lyrical prose; he ends on a splendidly poised and correctly balanced note of tenderness and faith and love; and then, having signed, sealed, and posted the missive, is suddenly overcome by the realization that by the very act of composition he has annulled the allure of the subject herself— cares no more about her, for the moment, than he does for an old piece of butcher's twine, which, all in all, is so alarming a discovery that he usually gets a little bit sick thinking about it, and has to go out somewhere and hear some music.

I have seldom met an individual of literary tastes or propensities in whom the writing of love was not directly attributable to the love of writing.

A person of this sort falls terribly in love, but in the end it turns out that he is more bemused by a sheet of white paper than a sheet of white bed linen. He would rather leap into print with his lady than leap into bed with her. (This first pleases the lady and then annoys her. She wants him to do both, and with virtually the same impulse.)

### UNCERTAINTY IN THE MIDDLE OF AN EMBRACE

There is no more disturbing experience in the rich gamut of life than when a young man discovers, in the midst of an embrace, that he is taking the episode quite calmly and is taking the kiss for what it is worth. His doubts and fears start from this point and there is no end to them. He doesn't know whether it's love or passion. In fact, in the confusion of the moment he's not quite sure it

## UNCONSCIOUS DRAWING: PLATE IV.

The mood captured in this drawing is a rare one indeed, and Dr. Karl Zaner considers the sketch the finest in his collection. Here the masculine sense of Ironic Detachment rises superior to the Love Urge and can take it or let it alone. The drawing was sent to Dr. Zaner by Mrs. Walter L. Mouse (née Kathleen Schaaf), recently divorced wife of the author of the drawing, Walter L. Mouse, of Columbus, Ohio.

isn't something else, like forgery. He certainly doesn't see how it can be love.

Let us examine this incident. He has been sitting, we'll say, on a porch with his beloved. They have been talking of this and that, with the quiet intimacy of lovers. After a bit he takes her in his arms and kisses her—not once, but several times. It is not a new experience to him; he has had other girls, and he has had plenty of other kisses from this one. This time, however, something happens. The young man, instead of losing himself in the kiss, finds himself in it. What's more, the girl to him loses her identity—she becomes just anyone on whom he is imposing his masculinity. Instead of his soul being full of the ecstasy which is traditionally associated with love's expression, his soul is just fiddling around. The young man is thinking to himself:

"Say, this is pretty nice now!"

Well, that scares him. Up to this point in the affair he has been satisfied that his feeling was that of love. Now he doesn't know what to think. In all his life he has never come across a character in a book or a movie who, embracing his beloved, was heard to say, "This is pretty nice," unless that character was a villain. He becomes a mass of conflicting emotions, and is so thoroughly skeptical and worried about the state of his heart that he will probably take to reading sociological books to find out if it's O.K. to go ahead, or whether, as a gentleman, it's his duty to step out before he further defames a sweet girl and soils her womanhood.

The medical profession recognizes two distinct types of men: first, the type that believes that to love a woman is not to desire her; second, the type that believes that to de-

*This peculiar posture was discovered by Dr. Tithridge in a patient who for thirty years, boy and man, had been unable to tell love from passion and who allowed it to prey on his mind. Drawings from the Tithridge collection of American male postures.*

sire a woman is not to love her. The medical profession rests.

This young man whom I've just mentioned (the rogue who found himself having a good time in the midst of a kiss) now takes seriously to books. Matters go from bad to worse. Hoping to find, in sexology, some explanation for his conduct which would indicate that, if not decent, it at least was not without precedent, he searches relentlessly until he comes upon a chapter on "The Theory of the Libido." (Note: it makes any young man a little mad to discover that he has a *pleasure-principle*, but there it is just the same.) On page 464 he finds this paragraph:

"The ideal healthy outcome is to find the child in whom the process of repression has been accomplished with no fixations of interest at lower stages of adaptation, in whom the Œdipus complex has passed into a 'normal' phase of the castration complex inhibition, and in whom a free movable libido is developing sublimation in active interests free from paralyzing inhibitions or anti-social tendencies."

This brings the young man to the point where he thinks maybe he better lay off altogether. He just wasn't cut out for kissing, he guesses. So he writes his girl a letter apologizing for having been a beast, breaks the engagement, and goes out to Oregon, where he raises fruit fairly successfully and with no anti-social tendencies.

I have taken up the question of Man's uncertainty about love and passion in two different circumstances—at the start of a letter, and in the middle of an embrace. It was originally my intention also to show how this uncertainty overcomes one *at the end of a day in the country* when a man is so tired that he not only can't distinguish love from passion, but has all he can do to distinguish one station on the New Haven railroad from another and often gets out at 125th Street by mistake. I say this was my intention; but thus far I have been so unsuccessful in explaining the difference between love and passion that to go on would be to lay myself open to criticism. The fact of the matter is, it's very difficult to tell love from passion. My advice to anyone who doesn't feel sure of the difference between them is either to give them both up or quit trying to split hairs.

# CHAPTER III

# A Discussion of Feminine Types

IN SPEAKING of the weaker sex in this book, the authors usually confine themselves to the generalization "Woman," "women," and "the female." For the larger discussions of sex, these comprehensive terms suffice. Yet no examination of the pitiable problem of Man and Woman would be complete without some effort to define a few of the more important types of the female. One cannot say, "Oh, well, you know how women are," and let it go at that. Many truths apply, and many foibles are common, to the whole sex, but the varieties of the female of the species are as manifold as the varieties of the flower called the cineraria.

Successfully to deal with a woman, a man must know what type she is. There have been several methods of classification, none of which I hold thoroughly satisfactory, neither the glandular categories—the gonoid, thyroid, etc. —nor the astrological—Sagittarius, Virgo, Pisces, and so on. One must be pretty expert to tell a good gonoid when he sees one. Personally, I know but very little about them, nor if I had a vast knowledge would I know what to do with it. It is even more difficult, and just as unimportant, to arrive at a zodiacal classification, because that is altogether dependent upon determining the year the woman was born, and because, even if you should ascertain her date of birth, the pishtosh of analysis and prediction which derives therefrom is a lot of mediæval guesswork. Or so it seems to

*"Successfully to deal with a woman, a man must know what type she is."*

me, and to Zaner, Blifil, Gorley, Peschkar, Rittenhouse, and Matthiessen.

Of much greater importance is a classification of females by actions. It comes out finally, the nature of a woman, in what she does—her little bag of tricks, as one might say.

A type of which one hears a great deal but which has never been very ably or scientifically analyzed, for the guidance of men, is the Quiet Type. How often one hears the warning, "Look out for the Quiet Type." Let us see if we should look out for it, and why.

The element of menace in the Quiet Type is commonly considered very great. Yet if one asks a man who professes knowledge of the type, why one should look out for it, one gets but a vague answer. "Just look out, that's all," he usually says. When I began my researches I was, in spite of myself, somewhat inhibited by an involuntary subscription to this legendary fear. I found it difficult to fight off a baseless alarm in the presence of a lady of subdued manner. Believing, however, that the best defense is an offense, I determined to carry the war, as it were, into the enemy's country. The first Quiet Type, or Q. T., that I isolated was a young woman whom I encountered at a Sunday tea party. She sat a little apart from the rest of the group in a great glazed chintz, I believe it was, chair. Her hands rested quietly on the chair arms. She kept her chin rather down than up, and had a way of lifting her gaze slowly, without disturbing the set of her chin. She moved but twice, once to put by a cup of tea and once to push back a stray lock from her forehead. I stole glances at her from time to time, trying to make them appear ingenuous and friendly rather than bold or suggestive, an achievement rendered somewhat troublesome by an unfortunate involuntary winking of the left eyelid to which I am unhappily subject.

I noted that her eyes, which were brown, had a demure light in them. She was dressed simply and was quite pretty. She spoke but once or twice, and then only when spoken to. In a chance shifting of the guests to an adjacent room to examine, I believe, some water colors, I was left quite alone with her. Steeling myself for an ordeal to which I am unused—or was at the time—I moved directly to her side and grasped her hand. "Hallo, baby! Some fun— hah?" I said—a method of attack which I had devised in advance. She was obviously shocked, and instantly rose from her chair and followed the others into the next room. I never saw her again, nor have I been invited to that little home since. Now for some conclusions.

Patently, this particular Q.T., probably due to an individual variation, was not immediately dangerous in the sense that she would seize an opportunity, such as I offered her, to break up the home of, or at least commit some indiscretion with, a man who was obviously—I believe I may say—a dependable family man with the average offhand attractions. Dr. White has criticized my methodology in this particular case, a criticism which I may say now, in all good humor, since the danger is past, once threatened to interpose insuperable obstacles, of a temperamental nature, in the way of this collaboration. It was his feeling that I might just as well have removed one of the type's shoes as approach her the way I did. I cannot hold with him there. Neither, I am gratified to say, can Zaner, but in fairness to White it is only just to add that Tithridge can.

However, the next Q.T. that I encountered I placed un-

*The Quiet Type.*

der observation more gradually. I used to see her riding on a Fifth Avenue bus, always at a certain hour. I took to riding on this bus also, and discreetly managed to sit next her on several occasions. She eventually noticed that I appeared to be cultivating her and eyed me quite candidly, with a look I could not at once decipher. I could now, but at that time I couldn't. I resolved to put the matter to her quite frankly, to tell her, in fine, that I was studying her type and that I wished to place her under closer observation. Therefore, one evening, I doffed my hat and began.

"Madam," I said, "I would greatly appreciate making a leisurely examination of you, at your convenience." She struck me with the palm of her open hand, got up from her seat, and descended at the next even-numbered street—Thirty-sixth, I believe it was.

I may as well admit here and now that personally I enjoyed at no time any great success with Q.T's. I think one may go as far as to say that any scientific examination of the Quiet Type, as such, is out of the question. I know of no psychologist who has ever got one alone long enough to get anywhere. (Tithridge has averred that he began too late in life; Zaner that he does not concur in the major premise.) The Quiet Type is not amenable to the advances of scientific men when the advances are of a scientific nature, and also when they are of any other nature. Indeed, it is one of the unfortunate handicaps to psychological experimentation that many types of women do not lend themselves readily to purposeful study. As one woman said to me, "It all seems so mapped out, kind of."

I am a little reluctant to report one other adventure with the Quiet Type, and that is why I seem to have summed up in the preceding paragraph without mentioning it. However, I now feel that some brief outline of the case I have alluded to should be set down here—especially after all this allusion. This young lady was a guest at a week-end party where I was also a guest. On Saturday evening it began to appear, quite early, that there was going to be considerable drinking. And, to be sure, there was. Among

*I asked her how I had reached the cliff—if I had walked there. "Partly," she said.*

those who became, as the fellow said, a little bit uncertain of themselves, were the young Q.T. and myself. It was, in all truth, largely her fault that I reached a state of abandon from which, at her further solicitation, it was but an easy step to a feeling of sheer devil-may-care. This condition, it is perhaps unnecessary to say, militates against that fine precision of mind so essential to the best results in any scientific investigation.

I do not remember all that ensued one-half so clearly as I should like to. I have often thought deeply on the matter, striving to reconstruct the complete scene, as it were, but my efforts have been hampered by the lamentable fact that I found dwelling upon the more easily remembered scenes so delightful that I simply dwelt on them. I remember, for example, that I was at the piano, or more exactly, on it—standing on it. The Quiet Type, fearing that I might fall, grasped me firmly about the knees, and I did fall. I was not only uninjured, but I got to my feet laughing. At this she began to laugh. I had lost my glasses in the fall, and began hunting for them. In bending over, however, I was assailed by a slight touch of vertigo, which runs in my family, and fell again.

The next that I remember is sitting on the edge of a cliff, or *falaise*, as the French call it, looking out over a lake. The young lady was beside me. "Well," she said, "what shall we do next?" I asked her how I had reached the cliff—if I had walked there. "Partly," she said. This set me to thinking. "I have lost my glasses," I said, and began hunting for them again. She again seized me by the knees, and I fell. In falling, both of us became enormously involved. I instantly arose and was about to step into the lake, when she grasped me around the waist. We both sat down. "You have gone as far as you can," she said, and tittered. "I should like to go a little farther," said I. She arose. "You're a funny man," she said, and laughed again. I grasped her, much to my surprise, by one ankle, and she began to topple toward the lake. I fell heavily backward, pulling her with me, and this doubtless saved her life. "You must be more careful," I told her. We sat up. "Don't you think you better take me home?" she said, in a singular voice—low and odd. "Rather," I responded, and arose. I took her back to

*The Buttonhole-twister Type.*

the house, which was some half-mile distant, we joined the others, and that is all I remember.

I shall always regret, of course, that I did not have full possession of my faculties during the walk to the cliff's edge, for there might have been, in the ten or fifteen minutes it must have taken, an excellent opportunity to "get at" the young woman. There is nothing quite so provocative of pleasant, revelatory talk as a quiet walk with some one at night. However, the episode ended as I have said, and a golden opportunity was lost.

In my very failures I made, I believe, certain significant findings in regard to the Quiet Type. It is not dangerous to men, but to a particular man. Apparently it lies in wait for some one individual and gets him. Being got by this special type, or even being laid in wait for, would seem to me in some cases not without its pleasurable compensations. Wherein, exactly, the menace lies, I have no means of knowing. I have my moments when I think I see what it is, but I have other moments when I think I don't.

The Buttonhole-twister Type is much easier to come at. A girl of this persuasion works quite openly. She has the curious habit of insinuating a finger, usually the little finger of the right hand, unless she be left-handed, into the lapel buttonhole of a gentleman, and twisting it. Usually, she picks out a man who is taller than herself and usually she gets him quite publicly, in parks, on street corners, and the like. Often, while twisting, she will place the toe of her right shoe on the ground, with the heel elevated, and will swing the heel slowly through an arc of about thirty or thirty-five degrees, back and forth. This manifestation is generally accompanied by a wistful, far-away look on the woman's face, and she but rarely gazes straight at the man. She invariably goes in for negative statements during the course of her small writhings, such as "It is not," "I am not," "I don't believe you do," and the like. This type is demonstrative in her affections and never lies in wait with any subtlety. She is likely to be restless and discontented with the married state, largely because she will want to go somewhere that her husband does not want to go, or will not believe he has been to the places that he says he just came from. It is well to avoid this type.

A charming but altogether dangerous type is the "Don't,

*I am told that one type has actually been known to get the man of her choice down and sit, as it were, side-saddle of him.*

dear" Type. By assuming a middle of the road, this way and that way, attitude toward a gentleman's advances, she will at once allure and repulse him. The man will thus be twice allured. He calls on her, and they sit in the porch swing, let us say. When he slips his arm around her, she will say in a low tone, "Don't, dear." No matter what he does, she will say, "Don't, dear." This type is a home-maker. Unless the man wants a home made for him within a very short time, it is better for him to observe the "don't" rather than the "dear," and depart. The type is common in the Middle West, particularly in university towns, or was some few years ago, at any rate. Any effort to classify modern university types would be difficult and confusing. They change from year to year, and vary with the region. I am told that one type has actually been known to get the man of her choice down and sit, as it were, side-saddle of him. I would not give even this brief mention, in passing, to college types of the female, were they not important because they so frequently divert a man from his career and tie him down before he has a chance to begin working, or even to say anything.

The rest of the types of American women, such as the Outdoors, the Clinging Vine, and so on and so on, are too generally known to need any special comment here. If a man does not know one when he sees it, or cannot tell one from another, of these more common types, there is little that can be done for him. No man should contemplate marriage, or even mingle with women, unless he has a certain measure of intuition about these more obvious types. For example, if a man could not tell instantly that a woman was the sort that would keep him playing tennis, or riding horseback, all afternoon, and then expect him to ride back and forth all night on the ferry, no amount of description of the Outdoors Type would be of any avail.

There is, however, one phenomenal modern type, a product of these strange post-war years, which will bear a brief analysis. This is the type represented by the girl who gets right down to a discussion of sex on the occasion of her first meeting with a man, but then goes on to betray a great deal of alarm and aversion to the married state. This is the "I-can't-go-through-with-it" Type. Many American virgins fall within this classification. Likewise it contains women who have had some strange and bitter experience about which they do a great deal of hinting but which they never clearly explain. If involved with, or even merely presented to, a woman of this type, no man in his right mind will do anything except reach for his hat. Science does not know what is the matter with these women, or whether anything is the matter. A lot of reasons have been advanced for girls acting in this incredible, dismayed manner—eleven reasons in all, I believe—but no one really knows very much about it. It may be their mothers' teaching, it may have been some early childhood experience, such as getting caught under a gate, or suffering a severe jolting up by being let fall when a boy jumped off the other end of a teeter-totter, or it may simply be a whim. We do not know. One thing is sure, they are never the Quiet Type. They talk your arm off.

# CHAPTER IV

# The Sexual Revolution:
# Being a Rather Complete Survey
# of the Entire Sexual Scene

THE sexual revolution began with Man's discovery that he was not attractive to Woman, as such. The lion had his mane, the peacock his gorgeous plumage, but Man found himself in a three-button sack suit. His masculine appearance not only failed to excite Woman, but in many cases it only served to bore her. The result was that Man found it necessary to develop attractive personal traits to offset his dull appearance. He learned to say funny things. He learned to smoke, and blow smoke rings. He learned to earn money. This would have been a solution to his difficulty, but in the course of making himself attractive to Woman by developing himself mentally, he inadvertently became so intelligent an animal that he saw how comical the whole situation was.

Thus, at the very start of the sexual revolution, Man faced one very definite problem: in becoming mentally

*"The lion had his mane . . . but man found himself in a three-button sack suit."*

"aware," he had become intellectually critical, and had discovered that it was increasingly difficult to make up his mind whether he really desired any one woman, however capable he was of getting her. It was the heyday of monogamy, and in order to contemplate marriage, it was necessary for a man to decide on One Particular Woman. This he found next to impossible, for the reason that he had unconsciously set up so many mental barriers and hazards.

Let me mention a few.

(1) The fear that his fiancée might get fat inside of a few years. To any mentally alert man, this thought was a strong deterrent. Quite often the man met the girl's parents. He would quickly size up her mother and make a mental calculation as to how long it would be before the daughter was in the same boat. Somehow, it took the bloom off the romance. If he was not fortunate enough to meet the parents of the young lady, he was quite apt to note things about her own conformation that seemed prophetic. A slight thickness in the neck, a trace of rotundity in the bosom, a touch too much ankle. In these portents he found much discomfort, and was quite likely to call the engagement off.

(2) The use of a word, phrase, or punctuation mark by his fiancée that annoyed him. In these early days of the sex awakening, it was not at all uncommon to find examples of the girl's using some slight phrase which had a grating effect. It was often the case that the man was literarily in-

clined—because literary inclinations were early found to be advantageous in sex, almost as advantageous, in fact, as the peacock's tail—and if this was the case the man was doubly sensitive to the curious little crudities, niceties, whimsies, and circumlocutions which women were afflicted with. I am thinking at the moment of the case of a young man who, in his junior year in college, had found the girl he believed ideal for him to marry, and then one day learned, quite by accident, that she was in the habit of using the word "Howdy" as a form of salutation. He did not like "Howdy," although he did not know why. Days and nights he spent trying to reconcile himself to the idea of it, weighing the young lady's extreme beauty and affability against her one flaw. In the end he decided he could not stomach it, and broke the troth.

(3) Difference in height. If a man fell in love with a woman taller than himself (which sometimes happened), he became morose from dwelling on the objections to such an alliance. This particular situation usually had a way of settling itself automatically: there were so many reasons, real or imaginary, why the man felt that the marriage was impossible, that just the mere business of thinking about them broke him in health and he died, leaving a margin of several weeks before the date of the wedding.

(4) The suspicion that if he waited twenty-four hours, or possibly less, he would likely find a lady even more ideally suited to his taste than his fiancée. Every man enter-

"*He would quickly size up the mother and make a mental calculation as to how long it would be before the daughter was in the same boat.*"

tained such a suspicion. Entertained it royally. He was greatly strengthened in his belief by the fact that he kept catching a fleeting glimpse of this imaginary person—in restaurants, in stores, in trains. To deny the possibility of her existence would be, he felt, to do a grave injustice to

*Male Type (eastern seaboard). Definitely interested in, but uncertain what to do about, the Female. To men of this type many aspects of the Sexual Revolution never became clear at all.*

her, to himself, and to his fiancée. Man's unflinching desire to give himself and everybody else a square deal was the cause of much of his disturbance. Man had become, you see, a thinking being. He had come to know enough about permutations and combinations to realize that with millions of Caucasian females to choose from, the chances of his choosing the ideal mate were almost zero.

So matters went. Man, we have seen, had begun to develop himself so that he would be attractive to Woman, and in doing so had made Woman of doubtful attraction to *him*. He had become independent. He had become critical. He had become scared. Sex was awakening and it was all Man could do to keep from laughing.

Woman, on her part, saw dimly what was going on in the world. She saw it through the sweet haze of Dream. She caught glimpses of it in the mirror of her Narcissistic soul.[1]Woman was at the crossroads. She had many ways open to her, but she chose one: *she chose to imitate Man.* At a time when sex was in transition, she had the bad judgment to begin a career of independence for herself, in direct imitation of her well-meaning mate. She took up smoking. She began to earn money (not much, but some). She drank. She subordinated domesticity to individuality —of which she had very little. She attained to a certain independence, a cringing independence, a wistful, half-regretful state. Men and women both became slightly regretful: men regretted that they had no purple tail to begin with, women that they had ever been fools enough to go to work. Women now "understood life," but life had been so much more agreeable in its original mystery.

And now we come to Sex.[2] Woman, observing that her mate went out of his way to make himself entertaining, rightly surmised that sex had something to do with it.

[1] This is the first mention in this article of Narcissism. You'll hear more about it, don't worry.
[2] Are you glad?

From that she logically concluded that sex was recreational rather than procreational. (The small, hardy band of girls who failed to get this point were responsible for the popularity of women's field hockey in this country, 1911-1921.) As though in a vision, the "right to be sexual" came to women. They fell to with a will. For thousands of years they had been content merely to be amiable, and now they were going to be sexual. The transition from amiability to sexuality was revolutionary.[1] It presented a terrific prob-

"Sex atrophied."

lem to Woman, because in acquiring and assuming the habits that tended to give her an equality with Man, she discovered that she necessarily became a good deal like Man. The more she got like him, the less he saw in her. (Or so he liked to think, anyway.) Just as soon as she began to put her own sex on an even basis, she found that he lost

[1] Zaner claims it was also amusing.

interest. Her essential Narcissism (pleasure of looking in a mirror) was met by his Begonia-ism (concept of the potted plant). Things got so that Woman spent *all* her time admiring herself in mirrors, and Man, discouraged, devoted himself quietly to raising begonias, which are fairly easy to raise. Sex atrophied.

But, as I say, sex was in the transition stage. Woman soon began to outgrow her Narcissism and was satisfied to snatch quick glances of herself in make-shift mirrors, such as the backs of watches, the shiny fenders of automobiles, plate-glass windows, subway weighing machines, and such. Convinced that sex was not sin, she set out joyously to study it. How hard she studied has recently been apparent, even to persons who read only a few books a year.

New York became the capital of the sexual revolution. It was conveniently located, had a magnificent harbor,[1] a high mortality rate, and some of the queerest-shaped apartments to be found anywhere. There are apartments in New York in which one must step across an open bathtub in going from the kitchen to the bedroom; any unusual layout like that arouses sexual desire and brings people pouring into New York from other cities. New York became the Mecca for young ladies from the South and from the Middle West whose minds were not quite made up about sexual freedom, but who thought that if they could

[1] New York has one of the finest harbors in the world.

once get to New York and into an irregular apartment, the answer might come to them.

Their mothers were against it.

"Now what can you get in New York that you can't get right here at home?" their mothers said.

"Concerts, new plays, and the opera," the daughters invariably replied. There has never, to my knowledge, been

"Furthermore, she was beginning to have Schmalhausen trouble."

a case of a young lady telling her mother that she wanted to go to New York because she was seeking an outlet for her erotic eagerness. It was always concerts that she wanted. Often it turned out to be concerts that she got.

When she arrived in New York and secured her unfurnished apartment (usually in West Fourth Street), her mental elation was so great and her activity in making parchment lamp shades so unabating that for the first couple of weeks she let sex go. Women are notoriously apt to get off the track; no man ever was diverted from the gratification of his desires by a parchment lamp shade. At any rate, the young lady was so tired at night she could hardly keep her eyes open, much less her mind. Furthermore, she was beginning to have *Schmalhausen* trouble. *Schmalhausen* trouble is a common ailment among girls in their twenties. It usually attacks girls who have taken a small apartment (*schmalhausen*) and are reading the behaviorism essays of Samuel D. Schmalhausen. The effect of sitting within narrow walls and absorbing a wide viewpoint breaks down their health. The pain that they suffer during this period is caused by their discovery of the lyrical duality, or two-sidedness, of life—a discovery that unbalances all sensitive young ladies in whom sex cries for expression. Even in a New York apartment there are two sides to everything, and this particularly applies to a girl's potential sexuality.[1]

Let me explain this duality.

The very fact that the young lady had settled in the vicinity of Sheridan Square indicates that there was a

---

[1] Girls with a bad case of Schmalhausen sometimes saw as many as three sides to sex.

strong vein of poetry in her. She saw life (and sex) through a lyrical haze which tended to accentuate its beauty by softening its truths. The whole purpose and scheme of poetry is to heighten the tenderness and essential goodness of life by a musical elaboration of its traditional worth.[1] Well, when the young lady allowed the lyrical possibilities of love to work on her mind, it made her mad to remember how candid she had been the night before in discussing contraception with the commercial artist who lived downstairs. It grew to be a big question in her own mind, just what her emancipation ought to consist of: whether it meant having lemon skins and gin stoppers in the washbasin and talking freely of exhibitionism and voyeurism, or whether it meant being the recipient of some overwhelmingly beautiful passion which her poetical soul still prescribed but which she knew couldn't exist because she was so widely read. To stall for time she would make another lamp shade.

Days slipped by. Always there was conflict in her soul. She had plunged into the "candor régime" whole-heartedly; she could enter a roomful of people and say almost anything at all. She also went in for nudity—another outlet for sex eagerness. She dallied in the bath, lay around the apartment without any clothes on, appeared scantily clad at her door when the laundryman called to collect, and week-ends went swimming naked in the moonlight with

[1] See Tithridge's "Poetry," but don't read it.

other young people. (Incidentally, when she saw what a man looked like without any clothes on, the old *Schmalhausen* trouble came back stronger than ever.)

By and by, because of this very uncertainty of soul, a kind of orderliness of habit crept into her life. Unable to decide whether sex was the poem she half believed it to be or the casual episode she had schooled herself to think it was, she compromised by practically giving sex the air. She now held a good job and was earning well. Candor and nudity, with an occasional bit of exhibitionism, began to satisfy her completely. She was growing older. The apartment was nicely decorated now and teeming with lamp shades. She held some good industrial stocks and had developed an ambition to write. She became content to be literary rather than sexual. She became, in other words, that most dangerous of all by-products of the Sexual Revolution—a biologico-cultural type. She had a way of leading young men on into exhilarating topics, and sitting with them in provocative attitudes, and then putting on her hat and going quietly home to bed. In short, New York was now home to this girl, this biologico-cultural lady, and she was in a fair way to step placidly into a good old-fashioned marriage when the right man came along.

And he usually did, the poor yap.

# CHAPTER V

# The Lilies-and-Bluebird Delusion

THE young bridegroom who unexpectedly discovers that his wife has been brought up in extreme unawareness of the true facts of life and believes in some variant of the Birds and Flowers Delusion (that is, that birds and flowers have something to do with the emotional life of persons), is faced with a situation calling for the greatest tact and tenderness. It won't do any good for him to get mad, or to indulge in self-pity, crying, "Oh, how sorry I am for me!" and only a coward would go directly into a psycho-neurosis without first trying to win his wife over to acceptance of things as they are.

I have in mind the case of a young lady whose silly mother had taught her to believe that she would have a little son, three years old, named Ronald, as soon as her husband brought a pair of bluebirds into a room filled with lilies-of-the-valley. The young woman (to say nothing of the young man) was thus made the victim of one of the extremest cases of Birds and Flowers Fixation which has ever come to my attention. I shall transcribe, from Dr. Tithridge's notes, the first dialogue on the subject that took place between the young couple. This dialogue was carefully reconstructed by Tithridge from the account of the incident as given by the young husband, who sought his advice and counsel.

On the evening of the 25th of June, when the couple were married, the young husband entered their hotel suite to find it literally a garden of lilies-of-the-valley. He was profoundly touched, but baffled, and asked his wife who was dead.

"Where are the bluebirds?" she replied, coyly.

"What bluebirds?" he demanded.

"The bluebirds," she said, blushing.

Unfortunately, but not unnaturally, the bridegroom did not know what the bride was talking about. What was of the extremest importance to her, was to her husband merely an idle whim, a shadowy fancy. Obviously, the young couple should have talked such matters over long before, but they hadn't, and there they were. He strove to change the subject, whistled, lighted cigarettes, for he was nervous enough the way it was, but she kept recurring to the bluebirds. His bewilderment became tinged with some alarm, for during their courtship he had put forth no great effort to examine into her mental capacity, and he was now assailed by the excusable suspicion that she was perhaps not exactly bright. He talked rapidly, apprehensively, of many things. Among the things he talked about were the

**DR. WALTER TITHRIDGE**

*(after the etching by Veerbluergen)*

St. Louis Cardinals (a baseball club). From there it was but an easy associative step for his wife to go back to the bluebirds again.

"Aren't you going to get any bluebirds?" she persisted.

"I don't know where the hell I'd get any bluebirds tonight," he said, rather irritably, "me not being Bo-Peep."

The nuclear complex was made right then and there. There was a long tense silence, after which the bride burst into bitter tears.

"Now, dear," said her husband, more reasonably, "let's try to get this thing straightened out. What are you talking about, anyway?"

"Sex—if you want to know!" she blurted out, and swooned.

Instead of getting her a glass of water, he excitedly phoned the room clerk, but became embarrassed once he had got him, and merely asked that a couple of blankets be sent up. It was, unfortunately, as I have said, June—and warmish. Thus when the wife revived sufficiently to become aware of her surroundings, the husband was standing above her holding a pair of blankets, and looking pale and warm.

"What are those for?" she demanded, suspiciously, for the notion had now formed in her own mind (Dr. Tithridge feels, and I agree) that she very likely had married a dementia præcox case. These mutual suspicions of mental inadequacy are common during the first year of any marriage, but rarely are they aggravated by factors so clearly calculated to upset the mental equilibrium as bluebirds at midnight and blankets in June. This husband and wife were drifting farther and farther apart. The solution to

"Mutual suspicions of mental inadequacy are common during the first year of any marriage."

their problem was becoming more and more remote, what with this setting up of involved artificial barriers, this almost fantastical beclouding of the issue. Dr. Tithridge tells me that he believes the young man's reason would have been permanently dethroned had he (Dr. Tithridge) tweeted or chirped like a bird[1] on the occasion of the husband's first visit to him.

[1] Experiments of this sort, calculated to determine the possible effects of tweeting, or chirping, in the case of a Birds Fixation, fall, of course, outside the province of the psycho-analyst, and not only is the legality of their practice questionable, but the value of the results obtained is highly doubtful.

When the wife beheld her husband standing there with the blankets, she demanded, again, "What are you doing with those blankets?"

"I get cold," he mumbled, and he proceeded to put the blankets on the shelf of a closet which already held several extra pair. He was, furthermore, decidedly warm, and kept patting his brow with a handkerchief.

"Let's go out and take a walk," suggested his wife, apprehensively. To this her husband very readily agreed. They were getting afraid to stay in the same room with each other, than which there is no other condition in the world more certain to break up a marriage. Out in the street, among people, they both felt safer, and they wandered to a bench in a fairly crowded park, and sat down.

"Where did you get the idea that birds have anything to do with us?" demanded the bridegroom.

"My mumsy,"[1] she said.

"Well," he said, "she deceived you."

"About what?"

"About what you're talking about."

"Sex?" she asked.

"That isn't sex, honey," he told her. "Birds and flowers are simply . . . they do not . . . that is, we could live all our life without them."

---

[1] Young women who allude to their mothers as "mumsy" almost invariably present difficult problems in adjustment. The word is a sentimentalization of the more common "mamma" and indicates a greater dependence upon maternal direction and supervision than may be expected in the case of young women who use the more familiar term.

"I couldn't," she said, and, after a pause, "I always feared you didn't want children."

"I do want children. I want you. You want me. Everything is going to be all right."

"How is it?" she demanded.

"In the first place," he began, pulling at his collar, "it's this way. Now here's the way it is. Now you take me . . . or take you, say. In the first place the girl, that is Woman . . . why, Woman[1] . . ." He lapsed into a profound silence.

"Well, go on," she prompted.

"Well," he said, "you know how women are, don't you?"

"Yes," she said, doubtfully.

"That's fine," he said, brightening, "Now women are that way, then——"

"What way?" she asked.

"Why, the way you are . . . from me . . . than I am, I mean." He made a vague gesture.

"I don't see what you mean," she said. Her husband gave a light laugh.

"Hell's bells, it's simple enough," he cried, suddenly, giving the light laugh again; "it's certainly simple enough. Now, here. We'll take Adam and Eve. There they were, all alone, see?"

[1] Explanations of natural phenomena in terms of the collective noun, particularly where the noun becomes capitalized in the mind of the person striving to explain, are almost never successful.

DR. KARL ZANER

"There were two bluebirds," said his wife.

"Not till after the flood, there weren't," he corrected her. "Well, he found out that there were certain essential differences—what you might call on purpose. I mean there must have been some reason. You can count on it that things like that just don't happen. Well, then, he simply figured it out—figured out the reason."

"For what?"

"For all this discrepancy. Obviously it just didn't happen. It couldn't just have happened. It had to make some sense—nature is like that. So he—so he finally—ah—what he did was tell her, see? I mean he asked her."

"Asked her what?"

"He simply asked her," said her husband in calm, almost cold tones,—"he simply asked her why she thought this was. Is there anything wrong in that? And so gradually they understood why it was. It's as simple as that!" He looked at her triumphantly.

"What are you talking about?" she demanded.

"Listen," he said at last, firmly. "Both of us speak a little French, and we might try it that way. I think I could explain better in French. Why, even little children, tiny girls, sing *Auprès de ma blonde* in France, and think nothing of it. It's just a nice, wholesome idea—*auprès de ma blonde* —and it sounds like poetry—but take it in English and what do you get?"

" 'Quite close to my blonde' . . ." answered his wife.

". . . 'Qu'il fait bon dormir,' " her husband hurried on.

" 'How good it is to sleep,' " she translated.

"Fine! Now you're talking."

"Go on," she said, "you're talking."

"Well, all right, but first I wanted you to see that there is no reason to get embarrassed, because everything is lovely in French. So don't mind my frankness."

"I don't," said the bride.

"All right," he began again, "Alors, now, *il y a quelque chose que vous avez que je n'en ai pas, n'est-ce pas?*"

"*Oui,*" she said.

"*Bon,*" he said. '*Alors, ça c'est naturel—ah—ça c'est bien naturel . . .*"

"*Par exemple,*" put in his wife, a little illogically.

"*Dites,*" he said, and after a great pause, "*Dites donc—dites vous——*"

"You should really use 'tu' and 'toi' and not 'vous,' " said his wife; "it's more intimate."

"All right," he responded. "Now, *tu as quelque chose, tu as . . . toi.*"

"*Comment?*" she demanded.

"I just don't know enough words," said the bridegroom, wretchedly. The bride put her hand on his arm.

"Let's try 'thee' and 'thou' in English," she suggested.

"That's not a bad idea," he said. "Well, all right. Now thee has——"

"Hath," she corrected.

"Thee hath certain—ah——"

EMOTIONAL CHARADES.
PLATE I.

"One young man every night tenderly placed, with much strange clucking, a basket near the hearth into which he had some expectation that a baby would be deposited by a stork."

"Differences," she supplied. "But isn't it 'thou hath'—or is it 'thee hath'?"

"To hell with it!" cried her husband. "In all thy life hast never been around, for Pete's sake?"

"Certainly, and thou—and you have no right to talk to me like that!"

"I'm sorry," said the young man. "I'm sorry." He rose to his feet. "Ye gods! to think this had to happen to me! Ah, well. Listen. I tell you what, I'll write it out for you. How about that? And if you don't like the idea, why, all right, I suppose."

It was the next day that the young husband, who had sat up all night in the hotel lobby, thinking and writing, visited Dr. Tithridge. I am happy to report that, as not infrequently happens in such cases, a solution was finally arrived at. However, in a great number of cases the difficulty is never overcome. The home becomes a curious sort of hybrid, with overtones of the botanical garden and the aviary. The husband grows morose and snappish, the wife cross and pettish. Very often she takes up lacrosse and he goes in for raising rabbits. If allowed to go on, the situation can become so involved and intricate that not all the analysts from the time of Joan of Arc down could unravel it. The problem is by no means any simpler where the wife is cognizant of things as they are and the husband is ignorant. I know of one young man who every night tenderly placed, with much strange clucking, a basket near the hearth into which he had some expectation that a baby would be deposited by a stork. (Plate I.) Another young husband constructed at considerable expense a water-lily pond in his back yard and fondly rowed about in it, twilight after twilight, searching for infants, laying his finger to his lip, making "tchk, tchk" noises at his wife, who watched him in profound amazement. In both these cases the wives were fine women of strong character, with a background of sturdy pioneer stock, and they soon put a stop to such charades, once they divined the curiously entangled Wish Motives behind them. It may be said, indeed, that young wives are more candid and direct in their explanations of natural phenomena than young husbands, when they have to be.

The existence of such deplorable ignorance is a sad commentary on the sentimentality of a nation which sets itself up to be frankly sexual. There is much reason to be hopeful, however. The future parents of the land will doubtless come straight to the point in matters of this sort, when talking with their children. The children of today will be the parents of tomorrow, and you know how the children of today are.

# CHAPTER VI

# What Should Children Tell Parents?

SO MANY children have come to me and said, "What shall I tell my parents about sex?" My answer is always the same: "Tell them the truth. If the subject is approached in a tactful way, it should be no more embarrassing to teach a parent about sex than to teach him about personal pronouns. And it should be less discouraging."

In discussing sex enlightenment for parents, first of all, definitions are needed. What do we mean by "parents"? Do we mean all adults who have had children? Do we mean adults who have had children, they knew not why? Or do we mean married people who have given birth to one or more offspring but have never gone into the matter very thoroughly? For the purposes of this article, it will be assumed that by "parents" we mean all adult persons permeated with a strong sense of indecency.

I have talked with hundreds of children about the problem of educating their parents along sex lines. So many of them have told me that they honestly tried to give their elders the benefit of their rich experience in life, but that the parents usually grew flushed and red and would reply, "Nice people don't talk about such things." It is true that a great gap exists between the generations. The fact that children are embarrassed to have their parents along when they are attending certain movies or plays is indicative of how hard it is to overcome the old fear of allowing one's elders to learn anything. A child never knows at what point in a play his uninformed old father will start to giggle. It is hard for children to break through and really come in touch with their elders. "Nice people don't talk about such things!" is the defense which old people put up against life itself, when they feel it crowding in all around their heads. Parents hesitate to discuss things calmly and intelligently with their children for two reasons: first, they have a kind of dread of learning something they don't want to know; and second, they feel that if they must learn anything at all they would like to be spared the humiliation of learning it from their offspring. Actually, middle age (and even senescence) is marked by a great curiosity about life. There is a feeling that life is slipping away quickly, and that it would be terrible to have the end come before everything in life has been revealed. The beauty of life, always apparent, implies a mystery which is disturbing right up to the bitter end. The spectacle of old men wistfully attending sex lectures (as they frequently do) suggests that the strong suspicion exists in them that somewhere they will hear the magic word by which human affairs will become clarified, somewhere they will glimpse the ultimate ecstasy. Children who allow their fathers and mothers, to whom they owe their very existence, to go on wondering about sex, are derelicts to duty.

*"One's father and mother are never too old to be told facts."*

If young folks lack the tact or intelligence requisite to enlightening their parents, the task should be intrusted to some one else. Yet it is hard to say to whom. A child should think twice before sending his father around to public school to secure sex information from his teacher. Women teachers, to borrow a phrase, are apt to be "emotionally illiterate." Many teachers have had no sex life and are just waiting for somebody like your father to show up.

One's father and mother are never too old to be told facts. Indeed, it is most unkind to keep them in ignorance and allow them to nourish the doubts and horrors of their imagination. The majority of parents pick up their knowledge of the facts of life from smoking-car conversations, bridge-club teas, and after-dinner speakers. They receive it from their vicious adult companions who are only slightly less ignorant than they are and who give them a hopelessly garbled version. They pick it up, too, from the gutter.

This matter of picking up information from the gutter is an interesting topic in itself. Quite the most remarkable case history that has come to my notice is that of François Delamater, a parent thirty years of age, who went deliberately to the gutter for his sex education. He had heard, as all people do hear some time or other, that sex can be learned from the gutter, so he set out to make a comprehensive survey of the gutters of eighteen large American cities. For a long time he found out nothing, although he was a very curious man. By a peculiar piece of fortune, however, he happened to be walking in Cincinnati one day and met a man who was leading a tame stork. The man was in the gutter. The stork carried in its bill a live baby, in swaddling clothes. Smelling a rat, Mr. Delamater stopped the man and inquired where the baby came from. The man replied that he didn't know.

Fig. 7. It is customary to illustrate sexology chapters with a cross section of the human body. The authors have chosen to substitute in its place a chart of the North Atlantic, showing airplane routes. The authors realize that this will be of no help to the sex novice, but neither is a cross section of the human body.

"For that matter," continued Mr. Delamater, "where does any baby come from?"

The man shook his head. Then he relented and told Mr. Delamater that he had merely been hired to lead the stork around the streets to advertise a moving picture called "Her Husband's First-born." The whole incident so confused the mind of the thirty-year-old parent that he eventually evolved the strange theory that babies are born within the father, an erroneous notion that dwarfed his emotions and modified his character.

It is of the utmost importance, in imparting sex knowledge to one's parents, that it be done in such a way as not to engender fear or anxiety. The phraseology should be chosen carefully, and efforts should be made to explain everything clearly but without the use of words which have a tendency to make old people nervous. The word "erotic" is such a word. When it is necessary to speak of Man's erotic tendencies, it is best to substitute another word. In the first place, an overwhelming majority of parents do not know the exact meaning of the word "erotic," and to know an *inexact* meaning is worse than nothing. Many are apt to confuse it vaguely with "exotic." I have known parents to go through whole books by authors like Havelock Ellis or Mary Ware Dennett without understanding a single paragraph, because they thought Man's "eroticism" referred to his desire to be in some foreign place like Spain. Those parents that actually do detect the difference between the sound of the two words will immediately become nervous, inattentive, and dispirited. They will make some excuse to leave the room, and will wander out, probably to the ice-box to get themselves a cold snack, which they will eat while in a sulky frame of mind. Later they will look up the word in the dictionary, but will forget it by the time they hear it again in conversation or read it in print. Furthermore, all their taste for sex will be gone.

Just what to tell parents is, of course, a vital question, not to be answered dogmatically. Before a child can conscientiously approach such subjects as pedestalism, the recessive knee, begonia-ism, frigidity in men, birth control, sublimation, and the swastika fixation, he must clear the boards. The simple phases of sex should be imparted in a direct manner: it is best to explain things in a matter-of-fact way, rather than resort to such cloudy analogies as birds and flowers. Strange to say, the habits of birds and flowers have done as little to clarify the human scene as almost any other two manifestations in nature. Further, there is always the danger, in setting up plant or animal life as an example, that one's parents will place a literal interpretation on things. I am thinking particularly of the case—which all sociological students know about—of Nina Sembrich, the fifteen-year-old high-school girl who attempted to impart knowledge to her father by telling him about bees. (Nina's mother was dead, or she would have told her too.) She traced, in rather minute detail, the

"Strange to say the habits of birds and flowers have done as little to clarify the human scene as almost any other two manifestations in nature."

renascence of earth in spring, the blossoming of the trees, the activity of the bees and their function in distributing the pollen, the fertilization of the seed and its growth during the warm languorous summer days, finally the fruition and harvest.

It was a beautiful story, redolent of orchards and sunny hillsides, instinct with life—a story that had a soporific effect on Mr. Sembrich, lulling him as the buzz of a bee lulls one in hot daisy fields. The upshot of it was that he gathered a rather strange impression from the narrative and somehow got the idea that to have babies you had to keep bees. He bought several hives, installing them in the little sitting room on the second floor, where Mrs. Sembrich had kept her sewing-machine when she was alive. The acquisition of the apiary further complicated matters for Mr. Sembrich by reason of the fact that bees themselves enjoy a rather extraordinary sexual scheme—theirs is a complex society, infinitely more diverting and harder to understand than our own. Observed by a slightly nervous person who is trying to profit by a simple analogy—as Mr. Sembrich was—bees are capable of causing the utmost confusion.

If you will recall what you know about bees, you will readily understand what I mean. In a colony of bees, certain individuals have no sex whatsoever; these are the "workers." The male bees are "drones." The queen (or "mother") bee develops her sexual character only after being arbitrarily chosen for the purpose, walled up, and fattened on special food. Mr. Sembrich marveled at these things.

Basing his hopes entirely on what he had seen, he made his first overt act, which was to give up his business (he was a merchant tailor) on the assumption that to be endowed with masculine characteristics one had to be a drone. In this, of course, he was justified to some degree; for it is quite true that very busy men rarely are fully equipped for a complete or happy sex life. Business men commonly find a vicarious gratification for their erotic nature in card index systems. Often, their satiable appetite for life is dissipated in the process of dictating a single sales letter. Only men who devote virtually their entire attention to love ever glimpse its full glory or experience its bewildering intensity. (And they make so little money they might just as well not.)

Mr. Sembrich, therefore, was not without justification in becoming a drone, since life was what he wanted to find out about. But it was when he undertook to fatten up a lady of his acquaintance into a "mother" that he ran into difficulties. He locked her in the kitchen and plied her with rich desserts. He even urged honey on her—a rather literal expedient even for a man in his mental condition. The lady not only failed to become a mother, but she took sick and died, surrounded by a group of Mr. Sembrich's "workers," whom he had hired to help feed her. With a dead woman in the kitchen and a lot of bees upstairs in the sitting room, the household became unbearable as a place to live and bring up his daughter Nina, so Mr. Sembrich fled, still ignorant of the essential knowledge of life.[1]

Another case, not exactly paralleling the Sembrich affair, is the case of two parents who failed to learn something to their advantage because they happened to be at

Sun fish (mola-mola)

dinner. It happened this way. Charles Updegraff had sent his son, Junior, to spend the summer at a boy's camp. There, in addition to learning how to swim, paddle, and make fires, Junior learned about sex, so that he returned home fine and brown and a credit to the Updegraffs. (The Updegraffs had swum, paddled, made fires, and so on, for generations.) Now, at Camp Whortleberry (that was the name of the camp) the authorities had adopted what is known as the "pet method" for imparting sex knowl-

[1] Sexually speaking.

edge to the boys. Each boy was given charge of a pet of some kind, and the pets were given *carte blanche*. Junior Updegraff drew a pair of sunfish. To augment the actual pet study, the boys were also given lectures by the camp

*"Young Junior had hardly been home an hour when he thought he would do his old man a good turn by telling him what he knew about sunfish."*

director, who knew in a general way what he was talking about. Thus, when the summer was over the boys' minds were full of a strange assortment of facts and oddments, some of them rather amusing. Young Junior had hardly been home an hour when he thought he would do his old man a good turn by telling him what he knew about sunfish. The Updegraffs were at table.

"Pop," he said, "do you want the low down on a sunfish?"

Mrs. Updegraff hastily interrupted. "Better wait till after dinner, son," she said.

(Note: parents have always been held back by the superstitious idea that it is wrong to learn anything while eating.)

*Sea Rover*

"What's the matter with right now?" asked Junior. "I was just going to tell Pop about our pet study course. I know a lot of things."

"Wait till we're through eating," said Mrs. Updegraff.

"Why should I? A mouse is an embryo twenty days, a lop-sided apple is that way because it's been fertilized only on one side, male animals grow bright colored in the mating season, and so it goes. Sunfish . . . "

"Junior!" said Mrs. Updegraff, sharply. "Not till after dinner. Sunfish can wait!"

"No they can't!" cried Junior, warming up to his subject. "The father sunfish makes the nest, then . . . "

"We don't want to hear about it," snapped Junior's mother. "Tell us about your canoe trips."

"I never went on no canoe trips."

"Why not?"

"Always was watching the sunfish."

The matter was dropped and the meal continued in silence. After dinner Mr. Updegraff, secretly very much interested, hung around in the hope that his son would again open up the subject of sunfish. The boy never did. He was only a child and children are easily discouraged.

I suspect that the church is responsible, in large measure, for the ideas of life now held by adults. Sex is still sin to the evangelical clergy. A kiss is thinkable only when sanctified by the church. A child who permits his parents to continue in the belief that the elevation of the soul depends on the renunciation of the flesh, is hardly doing his duty by them. Sometimes it may be advisable to quote to your parents from standard works on the subject of sex. Great care must be taken, though, to avoid abruptness, as far as possible. Thus there is some doubt in my mind whether a child ought to approach its mother on a hot afternoon when she is tired and bedraggled, and say to her: "Ma, under favorable conditions a husband and wife should remain sexually attractive to each other during the whole period of their sexual potency."

That's no way for a child to talk.

Some children have told me that instead of quoting from books they have tried leaving the books lying around, opened at pertinent pages. Even this failed to work in most cases. The mothers usually just picked up the book, dusted it,closed it, and fitted it neatly in some nearby shelf. They thought it was dusty.

Sea robin

# CHAPTER VII

# Claustrophobia, or What Every Young Wife Should Know

THERE is an erroneous impression current nowadays that sex is everything. It is similar to the psychological delusion common during the war years that the war would never end. Man is inclined to exaggerate the immensity of his chief preoccupation. Thus when the World War was in progress, men convinced themselves that there would never be anything else but war. Then the war ended, and Man was left, as it were, stranded. Used to a tremendous preoccupation, he had to have another. He turned to sex, out of sheer momentum, and overestimated its importance as he had magnified the immensity of war.

Sex is by no means everything. It varies, as a matter of fact, from only as high as 78 per cent of everything to as low as 3.10 per cent. The norm, in a sane, healthy person, should be between 18 and 24 per cent. In these hectic days, however, it is not unusual to hear even intelligent persons say, or imply, that sex is everything. This, of course, leads to the mistaken idea that a couple who are, so to speak, emotionally compatible, are going to be compatible in every other way. "Take care of sex, and the details will look after themselves," is the rule, in a manner of speaking. Nothing could be more stupid. A man and woman may be very, very happy emotionally and not get anywhere at all. There are many reasons for this, but none is more important than the inability of many a husband, otherwise normal, to become adjusted to a lack of freedom. Freedom is as essential and as primary an urge with a man as the loss of it is with a woman. A man grows up with the desire to be free and unfettered. The boy of six wants to play outside the house all the time. He doesn't even want to come into the house for his meals. On the other hand, little girls like to be in the house as much as they can. When dusk falls, the little boys are restless under the urge to be several blocks away, playing Go, Sheepy, Go, but the little girls want to be home putting their dolls to bed. Usually at least one of the dolls is ill and needs constant attention. Often it is necessary to force little girls to go outside and get some air and exercise, just as it is frequently necessary to use force to get little boys *into* the house. And even when girls do go outdoors, they have to be watched like a hawk or they will be playing house in the dog box or under the cellar door.

And yet, in spite of all this, women marry men without giving the serious chasm between their essential natures a thought. They think that a man wants a home. Well, he does, in a vague sort of way. Not so much a home, however, as a house. He likes to be able to say where he lives when he goes to vote, and things like that. But he doesn't want a home in the sense that a woman does, to potter around in. He has neither the same urge nor the same talent for hanging pictures and rearranging furniture. A woman, no matter how opposed she may become to housework, still gets a small thrill out of shifting things. It never wears off. She may be too tired to cook and insist on going out to dinner, but before she goes she would be willing, nay, glad, to put the Victrola where the davenport is and move the davenport over in front of the fireplace. One simple move like that is enough to alarm a man sufficiently to serve as the onset of a serious psychological or mental disturbance. Men don't stop to reason about individual moves. As soon as a woman calls on her husband to help her change the position of a couple of pieces of furniture, he instantly thinks the house is going to be torn up, as it was last spring, with carpets rolled up in the hall, and stepladders and buckets everywhere. This gives him a strange "boxed-in" feeling. If that feeling recurs too often, the husband may get claustrophobia. Claustrophobia is "a dread of being in an enclosed space, of living under conditions which would interfere with a speedy escape into the open."

Every young wife should know the first symptoms of claustrophobia, because, if taken in time, it can be cured, but if allowed to run on, deterioration sets in and may result in anything from benign stupor to complete paranoia. Once a husband gets into the outer rim of the paranoid and paranoic psychoses, he may easily run through all of them, and in the end simply be no good at all. The first symptoms are usually innocuous enough, and may consist of nothing more than a mere Amplification of Personality Without Signs of Conflict. (The symptoms listed herein are largely selected from Claudé's table.) But from there it is an easy step up to and including Logical Development of Delusions upon False Premises, Fragmentation of Personality, Dissimulation of Egocentricity, Looseness of Systematization, Exaggerated Feelings of Prejudice, Polymorphic Delusions, Ingenious Methods of Defense, Reticence, Recourse to Legal Measures, Apathy, Writing Letters to the Newspapers, and, finally, Diminution, or Total Loss, of Neuro-Vegetative Reflexes. There is nothing sadder than the spectacle of a once strong, firm-minded man no longer master of his neuro-vegetative reflexes, to say nothing of a hitherto well-integrated fellow in the throes of Fragmentation.

### AVOIDING THIS SAD STATE

There are various simple ways to avoid this sad state of affairs. Of course, where a husband and wife have plenty of money to begin with, and servants take care of all the details of household management, there is very little danger of claustrophobia. (There is always danger, even with money and servants, of dual personality, melancholia, and automatic writing, but not of claustrophobia.) In wealthy marriages, which are usually made for either financial or social reasons, the husband and wife see little, if anything, of each other, and the husband need have no fear of being boxed in at all. He is free to come and go at any time. But I am dealing with the typical American marriage, in which the wife runs her own home—builds it up around her husband—either because she has to, or because she wants to. A woman's desire to potter about her own home goes back a long way, so far back that the urge often remains when economic necessity no longer exists. Women like to do their own work. They even build up ingenious excuses for doing it, such as claiming that the maid or the handy man didn't do it right. This desire may not last for longer than the first three or four weeks of marriage, but that is ample time for the onset of claustrophobia. During that period a wife will concentrate on buying kitchen ware, painting chairs, selecting silver patterns, building bookshelves, etc., to the complete exclusion of everything else in life. The young husband, hearing all this tinkling and rattling and shoving going on around him, smelling paint, listening to hammering, etc., will begin at once to have a fear of being trapped or "caught." He will strive to get out of the house, and his wife should allow him to go. What she almost invariably does, however, is to

*"He will strive to get out of the house, and his wife should allow him to go."*

stop him and ask him to hold a piece of chintz or toile de Jouy up over the mantel so that she can see whether she likes it there. She won't like it there, and he then has to hold it, first high, then low, then in between, over a table in another part of the room. When this point is settled, he will likely be asked to hang a few pictures. Now a curious thing happens to many sensitive husbands when they are hanging pictures or holding things against walls. They get the impression that the walls are being made thicker, for the purpose of making it harder for them to get out—interfering with a speedy escape into the open. This is usually the beginning of the most dangerous of all hallucinations in claustrophobia cases—the Persecution Complex. The husband feels that he is not only being boxed in, but persecuted. If deterioration is allowed to set in, the delusion of persecution may attain astounding proportions, such as that the Masons or the Piano-makers are against him, or that former Vice-president Charles G. Dawes is trying to "get" him. A case history will show how this happens.

Case No. 22. *Personal History.* Normal birth and development. Born June 14, 1894. Had the usual childhood diseases with no sequelæ. No serious accidents or operations. Patient began school at the age of six, got along very well, graduating from high school at 18. Graduated from college at 22, and became an architect. He always held good positions with good salaries. Considered capable and efficient. Habits normal. Everything normal. Case married when he was 29.

*General Make-up.* Always considered keen, intelligent, amiable, and trusting. Liked outdoor activities, something of an athlete, with a strong urge to "get away by himself." Began to be suspicious shortly after his marriage. He frequently showed this suspicion in his work by complaining to his associates that his ability was not recognized, and intimating that he thought the elevators in the building had purposely quit stopping for him, so that he could not get out. Nervous. Jumpy.

*Mental Examination.* Patient was very keen, alert, but suspicious when brought under observation. His demeanor was self-assertive, but he was inclined to be anxious and restless. He demanded his immediate freedom of the physicians who were examining him, and was greatly frightened. "Let's get out of here!" he kept repeating to the doctors. He was allowed to depart, commitment to an institution not being thought necessary on the occasion of this first examination. Later the patient became violent. Would jump up from dinner table and cry, "Let's get out of this!"

*Causation.* When examined for causation, the patient at first talked guardedly, and then incoherently. "Look out for the water!" he would say, and, again, "You can't get out that way!" His physicians, unable to correlate his statements and his apprehensions, called in Dr. Damon Prill, the eminent New York psycho-analyst. "What have we here?" said Dr. Prill. "Patient," explained one of the doctors. "Look out for the water!" cried the patient. "Where did the water come from?" asked Dr. Prill, quietly. "From the drip-pan under the refrigerator," said the

*Onset of the boxed-in feeling.*

patient. "Ah yes," said Dr. Prill. "You can't get out that way!" cried the case. "Now, why is it that we can't get out that way?" asked Dr. Prill. "Because we are painted in," said the patient. "Painted in, eh?" asked Dr. Prill. "You heard me," said the patient. "Painted in, hammered in, pictured in, davenported in"—here he made a strange twisting gesture with both hands, leaned forward, and ended, in a confidential whisper— "rolled up in a rug!"

The reiteration of these incoherencies was all that Prill could get out of the patient, but it was enough to persuade him to question the man's wife. He made some interesting discoveries. It turned out that the wife, one day, had asked her husband to keep his eye on the pan under the refrigerator and see that the water did not overflow, while she went to a bridge tea. The husband was home, going over some important plans. He forgot the pan and the place was flooded. The ceiling in the apartment below fell. The woman in the apartment below went all to pieces. The patient's wife, returning from her tea, went all to pieces. The patient went all to pieces. Thus the hallucination formulated in his mind that being married and living in a house necessitated going to pieces. As for being "rolled up in a rug," that, it transpired, had actually happened to him also. One day, during a thorough cleaning of the house, which his wife was superintending, she ordered two burly men to roll up a rug, without noticing that her husband was on it at the time. He was accordingly rolled up in it and had considerable difficulty getting out. As for being "painted in," Prill established that the husband was also actually painted in on one occasion. He was in the bathroom shaving, and his wife did not know it. Thus she had a man paint the floors outside the bathroom, and when the husband opened the door to emerge, he couldn't get out without stepping on the paint. He was about to step on the paint, anyway, when his wife saw him. "Here, here!" she said, "you can't get out that way!" There was no other way out. "You'll simply have to stay in there till the paint dries," his wife told him, and he did.

Fig. 14.

Here we have that strange, alert furtiveness which instantly overtakes a man when he beholds a woman doing something which he does not thoroughly understand.

Prill explained to the wife what these inhibitions had done to her husband and that his condition was precarious. He stressed the importance of allowing her husband his freedom at all times, paint or no paint. The husband was then brought back into the home and was allowed to live a free, unfettered existence, coming and going as he pleased —always, however, under the discreet surveillance of Dr. Prill. With that perspicacity of psycho-mental cases, however, that almost second sight, the patient became aware that some one was snooping around, watching him, and one night he leaped out of bed, pulled open the door of a little-used closet, and there was Dr. Prill watching. The patient, who otherwise might have been cured, went instantly into the last stages of the Persecution Complex.[1]

The husband-patient began with the idea that he was being persecuted by the Detective Bureau of the Police Department and gradually enlarged his Apprehension Field until he believed he was also being persecuted by the Navy, the towns of Indianapolis and St. Louis, and the Box Manufacturers' Association. He whispered to doctors that a bearded man,[2] representing the Box Manufacturers, was following him around with a box and trying to catch him. Partly to avoid this imaginary menace, and also partly to stay off imaginary paint, the patient no longer walked on the floor, but on table tops, mantels, and so on, leaping

---

[1] This discovery of Dr. Prill in the closet is one of the few blots on the splendid record of psycho-analysis, and is most unfortunate.

[2] Dr. Prill wore a small, black beard.

around the room like an oriole. Unless watched, he would jump for the window-sills, and try to get out. He wrote to the Department of Justice at Washington, and finally to the President of the United States, protesting against the activities of the Order of the Eastern Star, the Railway Y.M.C.A., a Rev. W—, and the *New York Times*. The case was decreed hopeless in 1926. Later, the wife got a divorce and the husband seemed to improve. He was permitted to go to a ranch in Dakota, where he had a horse, a dog, and a pipe and was allowed to come and go as he liked. The last time I saw the patient, he was completely cured.

### PREVENTION OF NUCLEAR FEARS

Prevention of the nuclear fears which lead to such cases of claustrophobia should be quite simple. A wife should strive at all times to give her husband at least the *illusion* that he is free to come and go. She should remember that it is the little things that count, that claustrophobia is brought on by an accumulation of small details, that it is, in fact, a tragedy of the trivial. If a husband uses a guest towel, he should be quietly reprimanded, but under no circumstances sent to his room. After pointing out, briefly, that the guest towels are not to be used, the wife might even give him a piece of bread and butter with sugar on it, or a kind word. Too many wives do not consider it important to explain the facts of the guest towel to their hus-

*A wife should tell her husband in clear, simple language where guest towels come from.*

bands. A wife expects her husband to pick up his knowledge in the gutter or from other husbands, who know as little about the actual truth as he does himself. If a husband uses a guest towel, he should be gently reproved and then told where guest towels come from, in clear, simple language. The wife should lead him to the drawer where she keeps the guest towels and show him wherein they differ from ordinary towels—the kind he may use. The average guest towel can be identified by curious markings, either elaborate initials or picturesque designs in one corner or running all the way around the border. The husband should also be told that the use of such towels is not pleasurable, because of the discomfort caused by the hemstitching, the rough embroidery, and the like. He should be made to understand that no man ever uses a guest towel, either in his own home or when he is a guest somewhere else, that they are hung up for lady guests to look at and are not to be disturbed. If he is told these simple truths in a calm, unexcited way, the chances are that he will never use a guest towel again and that he won't worry unduly over the consequences of his having used one once or twice. But as soon as he is given the idea that he has done something terrible, that old feeling of being boxed in comes over him. He begins to think that he will never do anything right around the house, and that his home is merely a laboratory in which he has been trapped for the purpose of serving as the subject of strange experiments with towels and furniture.

The same rules should apply to husbands when they leave things lying around, or track in dirt, or forget to shut the refrigerator door. None of these faults is, after all, of very great importance, and they should be lightly dismissed. If they are presented as heinous crimes, the husband is going to be liable to the inception of a Persecution Complex and the slow deterioration of mind and spirit incident upon claustrophobia. A wife is forever taking it for granted that her husband should know as much about a household as she does. If she would only realize that things which are easy and uncomplicated to her are strange and mysterious to her husband, and explain the mysteries to him, adjustments could be arrived at very simply, and sex would then have a chance to mean something. As an instance of what I mean take what happens during the average unpacking. A couple has just moved from one house to another, say, and the husband has been asked to help put things away. (He should not, of course, be asked, for the danger of that boxed-in feeling, with all of its awful consequences, is inherent in such a request.) As the things are taken out of trunks, the wife knows instantly where they go, not only the things she is going to use and wants put where she can get at them, but the things for which she has no immediate use and wishes stored away for the winter or summer, as the case may be. A woman can tell instantly whether a given article belongs in the attic or in the basement. All objects fall into one or the other of these two categories. For example, while I myself am not an expert at it, I am aware that anything framed or having wire attached to it goes to the attic, and that most containers and the like, especially those made of metal, go to the basement. A woman comes naturally by this ability to discriminate. She knows most of it by intuition and the rest she has learned from her mother. But to suppose that a husband should know, offhand, whether a chest of drawers with woolens or dimity in it goes to the attic or the basement is ridiculous. You might as well expect him to understand, without long, careful instruction, why one tea towel is used for the china and another for the glassware. The thing for a wife to do, then, is not to upbraid or rebuff her husband when she finds him tired and worn in the attic, sitting among a lot of things that should have been taken to the basement, but simply to say nothing, or, better yet, compliment him on his strength and agility and then, next day, hire a handy man to shift the things to where they belong. Adherence to a few simple rules of solicitude and understanding would prevent nine husbands out of ten, no matter how passionately dedicated to liberty they may be, from falling victims to the dread claustrophobia which every year takes its heavy toll of male minds as the result of the carelessness or stupidity of wives.

## CHAPTER VIII

# Frigidity in Men

I HESITATE to approach the subject of male unresponsiveness. Frigidity in men is a theme sociologists have avoided. Frigidity in women, on the other hand, forms a vast chapter in the sex research of today; the part it plays in marital discord is known to students of sociology as well as to the lay reader, although probably less well. It has occupied the attention of many noted writers, and has taken the lives of such men as Zaner and Tithridge, who carried some of their experiments too far.[1]

Any discussion of frigidity in men calls for an unusual degree of frankness on the part of the writer, since it entails such factors as the "recessive knee," Fuller's retort, and the declination of the kiss. Further, before attacking this subject, it will be necessary to reëvaluate some of the more fundamental hypotheses of Man's erotic nature, and what a nuisance that is going to be!

Let us go back a little way. There are two fundamental urges in nature: the desire to eat and the desire to reproduce one's kind. Which of these two impulses is the

[1] Tithridge especially.

stronger depends somewhat on the individual and somewhat on the circumstances surrounding the individual—that is, it is apt to vary with the quality of the food and of the women. There are, Zaner shows, men who would rather eat than reproduce, and there are isolated cases of men who would rather reproduce than eat. But it is the less simple types that provide the important case histories for the student of masculine frigidity, and no broad conclusions can be drawn about the relative merits of eating and reproducing without a consideration of the contributing factors.

Quite regardless of which urge comes first in Man's scheme of existence, it is safe to state dogmatically that the second urge (the "sex" urge) has caused more stir in the last few years than the first, or "nourishment," urge. Sex is less than fifty years old, yet it has upset the whole Western World. The sublimation of sex, called Love, is of course much older—although many purists will question the existence of Love prior to about 1885 on the grounds that there can be no sublimation of a non-existent feeling. What I shall try to show, without carping, will be that there is a very good reason why the erotic side of Man has called forth so much more discussion lately than has his appetite for food. The reason is this: that while the urge to eat is a personal matter which concerns no one but the person hungry (or, as the German has it, *der hungrig Mensch*), the sex urge involves, for its true expression, another individual. It is this "other individual" that causes all the trouble.

Except in rare instances, all of which have been dealt with by Sumner, the urge involves an individual of the

*"Just the minute another person is drawn into some one's life, there begin to arise undreamed-of complexities."*

opposite sex; that is, for a man it involves a woman, and for a woman it involves a man. I use the word "involve" advisedly. *Just the minute another person is drawn into some one's life, there begin to arise undreamed-of complexities,* and from such a simple beginning as sexual desire we find built up such alarming yet familiar phenomena as *fêtes, divertissements,* telephone conversations, arrangements, plans, sacrifices, train arrivals, meetings, appointments, tardinesses, delays, marriages, dinners, small pets and animals, calumny, children, music lessons, yellow shades for the windows, evasions, lethargy, cigarettes, candies, repetition of stories and anecdotes, infidelity, ineptitude, incompatibility, bronchial trouble, and many others, all of which are entirely foreign to the original urge and way off the subject, and all of which make the person's existence so strangely bewildering that if he could have foreseen these developments his choice would have been the "eating" urge, and he would have just gone quietly out somewhere and ordered himself a steak and some French fried potatoes as being the easier way out.

Still, that is just a hypothetical alternative. Life, as we know, is very insistent; almost daily people become involved with other people. And that brings us to our real theme, namely, frigidity in men.

*The Recessive Knee.* The first symptom of frigidity in men is what I call the recessive knee. To the study of this phenomenon I have given some of my best years. My laboratory has been the laboratory of life itself. Probably I would never have discovered the recessive knee had I not noticed it, some ten years ago, in myself. Questioning my colleagues, I found to my amazement that they too had had similar experiences which they were unable to account for, and this led me to continue my investigations. Since then I have gone into taxicabs, terminal lunch rooms, boat liveries, and all other places where it is possible or usual for a girl to let her knee rest lightly against that of her companion, have gained the confidence of the young men and women whom I was watching, and have accumulated a

*"Occasions arise sometimes when a girl presses her knee, ever so gently, against the knee of the young man she is out with."*

mass of data showing that frigidity in men, instead of being almost a nonexistent characteristic, is one of the commonest attributes of our national sexual life. Inasmuch as the juxtaposing of the knee by the female, which causes the recessive (or "pulled away") knee in the male, usually occurs fairly soon after dinner, my experiments and observations have had to be made largely in the evening. It has been my custom to sleep late mornings to make up for this.

Simply stated, the knee phenomenon is this: occasions arise sometimes when a girl presses her knee, ever so gently, against the knee of the young man she is out with. The juxtaposing of the knee is brought about by any of a thousand causes. Often the topic of conversation has something to do with it: the young people, talking along pleasantly, will suddenly experience a sensation of compatibility, or of friendliness, or of pity, or of community-of-interests. One of them will make a remark singularly agreeable to the other person—a chance word or phrase that seems to establish a bond between them. Such a remark can cause the knee of the girl to be placed against the knee of the young man. Or, if the two people are in a cab, the turning of a sharp corner will do it. In canoes, the wash from a larger vessel will bring it about. In restaurants and dining-rooms it often takes place under the table, as though by accident. On divans, sofas, settees, couches, davenports, and the like, the slight twist of the young lady's body incident to receiving a light for her cigarette will cause it. I could go on indefinitely, but there is no need. It is not a hard push, you understand—rather the merest touch of knee to knee, light as the brush of a falling blossom against one's cheek, and just as lovely.

Now, a normal male in whom there are no traces of frigidity will allow his knee to retain its original position, sometimes even exerting a very slight counter-pressure. A frigid male, however, will move his knee away at the first suggestion of contact, denying himself the electric stimulus of love's first stirring. Why? That is what my research was conducted to discover. *I found that in 93 per cent of all cases, the male was suspicious; in 4 per cent he was ignorant, and in 3 per cent he was tired.* I have presented these figures to the American Medical Association and am awaiting a reply.

It is the female's subtlety in her laying-on of the knee that annoys the male, I found. His recession is for the purpose of reassuring himself of his own integrity and perspicacity. If the female were to juxtapose in a forthright manner, if she were to preface her gesture with the remark: "I am thinking of letting my knee touch yours for the fun of it, Mortimer," she might gain an entirely different response from the male.

Many men with recessive knees have confided to me that they felt incapable of answering the pressure because of the effect it might have on their minds, with the accompanying loss of self-respect. I have established the fact that no *physical* detriment is incurred by answered pressure—the only harmful effects are psychological. Some males admitted to an unwillingness to give any woman the satisfaction of believing that she was able to take her companion unaware. Still others told me that they feared the consequences of such an act: they were afraid that if ever they let down the bars and failed to turn away from knee pressure, they would likewise be unable to resist other juxta-

"Many men have told me that they would not object to sex were it not for its contactual aspect." (One such man is shown in the background.)

positions in life and would continually be responding amiably to other amusing stimuli—sales talks, stock promotion, and the like.

It was a young Paterson, N. J., girl by the name of Lillian Fuller who let drop the remark that has epitomized, for the sociological and anthropological world, the phenomenon of the recessive knee. "Fuller's retort" is now a common phrase in the realm of psychotherapy.

Miss Fuller was an unusually beautiful woman—young, accurate, sensitive. She was greatly attached to a man several years her senior in the buffing department; wanted to marry him. To this end she had laid her knee against his innumerable times without a single return of pressure. His frigidity, she realized, was gradually becoming prejudicial to his mental health, and so one evening, after experiencing for the hundredth time the withdrawal of his knee, she simply turned to him with a quiet smile playing on her face and said, "Say, what is the matter with you, anyway?"

Her retort somehow summed up the whole question of frigidity in men.

*The Declination of the Kiss.*[1] Many men have told me that they would not object to sex were it not for its contactual aspect. That is, they said they would be perfectly willing to express their eroticism if it could be done at a reasonable distance—say fifty paces. These men (the frigid-*plus* type) found kissing intolerable. When they had

[1] Now we're getting down to business.

an opportunity to kiss a young lady, they declined. They made it plain that they would be willing to blow a kiss across the room from their hand, but not execute it with their lips.

*"Love had a simple directness which was not disturbed until the arrival, in the land, of the minnesingers."*

I analyzed scores of these cases, questioning both the women and the men. (The women were mad as hornets.) I found that a small number of the kiss-declining men were suffering from a pathology of the eyes—either astigmatism or farsightedness—so that when they got really close to a girl, she blurred on them.[1] The vast majority of

[1] Incidentally, I might say that this blurring of the female before the eyes of the male is not entirely unpleasant. It's kind of fun.

cases, however, were quite different. Their unwillingness I traced to a much subtler feeling than eye-strain. Your true anti-contactual, or kiss-decliner, is a very subtle individual indeed.

In effect, his is a throw-back to another period in history, specifically to the Middle Ages. He is a biological sport. (Note: this is very confusing, calling him a "sport," because the ordinary "sport" is not a kiss-decliner at all—anything but. Please keep in mind, then, that when I use the term "sport" I want the strict biological interpretation put upon the word. I want it, and I intend to get it. If there are any of you who think you are going to find the use of the word "sport" in this connection so confusing as to make the rest of the chapter unintelligible, I wish you would drop out. Get something else to read, or, better yet, get some exercise.)

No one can quite comprehend the motives and the successes of a kiss-decliner who does not recall his counterpart in mediæval history. In the Middle Ages, when men were lusty and full of red meat, their women expected as much. A baronial fellow, finishing his meal, made no ado about kissing a Middle Age woman. He just got up from the table and kissed her. Bango, and she was kissed. Love had a simple directness which was not disturbed until the arrival, in the land, of the minnesingers. It got so no baronial hall of the Middle Ages was free from these minnesingers. They kept getting in. They would bring their harps with them, and after dinner they would twang a couple of notes and then sing a frail, delicate song to the effect that women should be worshiped from afar, rather than possessed. To a baron who had just drunk a goblet of red wine, this new concept of womanhood was screamingly funny. While he

Mediæval baron, amused at minnesinger's concept of Woman.

was chuckling away to himself and cutting himself another side of beef, his wife, who had listened attentively to the song, would slip out into the alley behind the castle and there the *minnesinger* would join her.

"Sing that one again," she would say.

"Which one?"

"That one about worshiping me from a little distance. I want to hear that one again."

The *minnesinger* would oblige. Then he would illustrate the theme by *not* kissing the woman, but dancing off lightly down the hill, throwing his harp up into the air and catching it again as he went.

"What a nice young man," the baron's wife would think, as she slowly turned and went in to bed.

The kiss-decliner of today is a modern *minnesinger*. He is a sport in that he has varied suddenly from the normal type—which is still baronial. Of course, the amusing thing about his conduct is that oftentimes a woman assumes that she is being worshiped from afar, when as a matter of fact she is merely being *ignored from afar*. That is part of the trick of an anti-contactual person—he takes a perverse delight in allowing the woman whose kiss he had declined, to think of him as more lyrical than other men. When he leaves her presence, she is apt to think of him as off somewhere by the bank of a stream, lying flat on his back, his shaggy head buried in the tall grasses, dreaming of something or other (probably of her), whereas, if she would take the trouble to go to the nearest Liggett's drug store she would probably find him there, getting a sundæ.

By the mere gesture of declining a kiss a man can still make quite a lot of ground, even in these depleted days. The woman thinks: "He would not dream of embracing my body; now that's pretty white of him!" Of course, it would be wrong to ascribe motives of sheer deliberateness to the frigid male. Often he is not a bad sort—merely is a fellow who prefers an imagined kiss to the real kind. An imagined kiss is more easily controlled, more thoroughly enjoyed, and less cluttery than an actual kiss. To kiss in dream is wholly pleasant. First, the woman is the one of your selection, not just anyone who happens to be in your arms at the moment. Second, the deed is garnished with a little sprig of glamour which the mind, in exquisite taste, contributes. Third, the lips, imaginatively, are placed just so, the right hand is placed just so, the concurrent thoughts arrive, just so. Except for the fact that the whole episode is a little bit stuffy, it is a superior experience all round. When a kiss becomes actual anything is likely to happen. The lips, failing of the mark, may strike lightly against the end of the lady's nose, causing the whole adventure to crack up; or the right hand may come in contact with the hard, jagged part of the shoulder blade; or, worst of all, the man's thoughts may not clothe the moment with the proper splendor: he may be worrying about something.

So you see, frigidity in men has many aspects, many angles. To me it is vastly more engrossing than frigidity in women, which is such a simple phenomenon you wonder anybody bothers about it at all.

# Answers to Hard Questions

[Note: These questions have been selected from among the many thousand inquiries that were received by Dr. Karl Zaner during the past year. They come from people who are sexually inquisitive—people from every walk of life. The authors wish to thank Dr. Zaner for allowing them to have access to his sex files. It is with a sense of high adventure that we face the task of answering, to the best of our ability, these perplexing questions that deal so intimately with human lives.—THE AUTHORS.]

*Q. My youngest boy, age 28, turned against love because in a book he was reading, where the writer meant to say, "A woman in love is sacred" there was a misprint and it came out, "A woman in love is scared." How would you go about this?*

A. We do not regard the case as typical. Presumably your boy is badly frightened himself, or he wouldn't be reading books; he would be out somewhere. The way to overcome this is to build up his general health.

*Q. Should a woman live with her husband if they are separated?*

A. Yes. There is nothing that brings two people so close together as separation. In situations of the sort, the woman's presence gradually becomes necessary on account of the condition of the man's shirts. On first being separated from his wife, the husband commonly will be found to

*"On first being separated from his wife, the husband commonly will be found to neglect his dirty clothes, from spite and from self-indulgence. Instead of gathering them into a pile and sending them to the laundry, he will put on yesterday's shirt in the morning, and stop in a gentlemen's furnishing store to pick up a clean one on the way to the office."*

neglect his dirty clothes, from spite and from self-indulgence. Instead of gathering them into a pile and sending them to a laundry, he will put on yesterday's shirt in the morning, and stop in a gentlemen's furnishing store to pick up a clean one on the way to the office. This procedure has a threefold allure for the man. First, it gets him to the office half an hour late; second, it takes him into a furnishing store; and third, when he looks into his shirt drawer in the morning and finds no shirts it assures him of the disorganized state of his life. To feel disorganized is to be perfectly happy.

Things might go on this way indefinitely were it not for the economic side of the question. At three dollars a shirt (which is a conservative figure for a man separated from his wife) the shirt bill runs into eighteen dollars a week, plus another six dollars for underwear and socks. Furthermore, there is now a congested condition in the husband's office, caused by the accumulation of dirty shirts which he has tucked into bottom drawers and filing cabinets. This shows up in his work.

The impracticability of two people living apart becomes apparent, too, in the matter of the old 1916 Cadillac touring car which they own. On separating, the husband will generously give the car to his wife to use, but that doesn't alter the fact that he, and he alone, knows what you have to do when the car "does that funny thing." Thus, the husband is apt any time during the day to pick up the phone and hear his wife's voice:

"Dear, I'm on the Merrick Road between Bellport and Patchogue, and the car is doing that funny thing again." This means dropping whatever work he is doing, taking a cab to the Penn station and a Long Island train to the scene of the breakdown. This also shows up in his work.

It never could happen if husband and wife were living together, because in that case they would never be on cordial enough terms for him to let her use the car.

There is another phase of separation that is perhaps more alarming than those we have mentioned, namely the possible effect the news of it might have on the health of the wife's parents or the health of the husband's parents. I recall the case of a couple who over a period of years tried to live apart without telling the wife's mother—who had a frail heart and who liked to see young people together, not apart. (Note: old ladies don't know *why* they like to see young people together—they can give no reason; yet just the thought of two young people separating excites them unduly, and, when their heart is unreliable, is apt to carry them off.) So this young pair, out of consideration, although separated, sent community Christmas presents to the parents and wrote letters describing joint experiences, until, after two years and eight months of struggling along and scheming, they finally gave up the battle and decided it would be simpler to take an apartment together somewhere. Sheer fatigue united them. They are residing, to this day, in North Pelham, and the wife's mother is still alive and well. Getting better every day, doctors say.

So our advice to any couple is just this: separate if you must, but by all means live together—no matter how your friends and neighbors talk.

*Q. I have an aquarium and I got a snail for it because they told me it would keep the water clean, and the snail unexpectedly bore young, although it was in there all alone. I mean there weren't any other snails in there, only fish. How could it have young, very well?*

A. The snail in your aquarium is a mollusc. It is quite likely an hermaphrodite, even though it came from a reputable department store. For being hermaphroditic, nobody can blame a snail. We cannot tell you everything we know about the gastropods because we know, possibly, more than is good for us. In the absence of specific information to the contrary, we would say that the snail in your aquarium had been going around a good deal with other snails before you got him (her). Some molluscs (not many) can have children merely by sitting around and thinking about it. Others can have children by living in a state of reciprocity with other hermaphrodites. Still others are like us, diœcious, possessed of only one sexual nature but thankful for small favors.

The shellfish and the snails are a great group, though it is a pose with many people to consider them dull. Usually the people who find molluscs dull are dull themselves. We have met molluscs in many parts of the world: in gardens in France, on the rocks at low tide on Long Island Sound, in household aquaria, on the sidewalks of suburban towns in the early mornings, in restaurants, and in forests. Everywhere we found them to be sensitive creatures, imaginative and possessed of a lively sense of earth's pleasant rhythm. Snails have a kind of nobility. Zoölogists will tell you that they occupy, in the animal kingdom, a position of enviable isolation. They go their own way.

We can understand your curiosity about sex in snails. Molluscs are infinitely varied in their loves, their hates, and their predilections. They have a way of carrying out ideas they get in their head. They are far from cold, as many people suppose them; indeed, one of the most fascinating love stories we ever read was in the *Cambridge Natural History*, in which was described the tryst kept by a pair of snails on a garden wall. We have never forgotten the first sentence of that romantic and idyllic tale, nor have we forgotten the name of the snail, L. Maximus. The story started: "L. Maximus has been observed at midnight to ascend a wall or some perpendicular surface." It then went on to relate how, after some moments spent greeting each other, crawling round and round, the snails let themselves down on a little ladder of their own devising, and there, suspended in the air ten inches or so from the top of the wall, they found love.

Often very fecund, molluscs are rarely too busy to give attention to their children after birth, or to prepare for their coming. There is, in Algeria, a kind of mollusc whose young return for shelter to the body of their mother, somewhat in the manner of little kangaroos. There is, in the

Philippines, a snail who is so solicitous for her expected babies that she goes to the trouble of climbing, with infinite pains and no little discomfort, to the top of a tall tree, and there deposits her eggs in a leaf, folding the leaf adroitly for protection. Another kind of mollusc, having laid her eggs upon a stone, amuses herself by arranging them like the petals of a rose, and hatches them by holding her foot on them. Molluscs tend to business.

Sometimes different species intermarry, but this is rare. The interesting point about it is that such unions generally take place when the air is heavily charged with electricity, as before a storm, or when great rains have made the earth wet. The Luxembourg Garden in Paris is a place snails go to for clandestine matches of this sort. H. Variabilis goes there, and Pisana. The moisture, the electricity, the fragrant loveliness of a Paris night, stir them strangely.

Probably, if you know so little of the eroticism of snails, you have not heard of the darts some of them carry—tiny daggers, hard and sharp, with which they prick each other for the excitement it affords. These darts are made of carbonate of lime. The Germans call them *Liebespfeil*, "love shaft." Many British molluscs are without them, but that's the way it goes.

We could tell much more. We could tell about molluscs that possess the curious property of laying their eggs on the outside of their own shell, and of the strange phenomenon of the Cephalopod, who, when he takes leave of his lady, leaves one of his arms with her, so that she may never lack for an embrace. But we feel we have answered your question.

# Glossary

AARON'S DISEASE: Put in here merely because it might confuse the reader if we started right off with Admiral Schley.

ADMIRAL SCHLEY: American naval hero in whose splendid achievements men took an interest when their absorption in love died down, *circa* 1900.

AMATORY INSTINCTS: Interest in sex.

APATHY: Almost total loss of interest in sex.

ATROPHY: Total loss of interest in sex.

ATTACK: Man's method of showing interest in women, so called because of his brusque desire to get at the matter in hand and have done with it.

BEGONIA-ISM: Tendency of the male to raise small potted plants, and not go out.

BENIGN STUPOR: Alarming condition in a husband or lover which causes him to sit around in his bathrobe and slippers, brooding, instead of working or anything.

BIOLOGICO-CULTURAL: A feminine type; one who expresses her erotic nature verbally.

BOTHER: Annoyance; frequently confused with "pother," which means uncalled-for interest in something, usually sex.

BOXED-IN: Caught, or trapped, as a husband by a wife, or the delusion of being caught or trapped.

BUTCHER'S TWINE: A kind of stout cord of no particular interest to anybody.

CAUSATION: The factors back of a male's doubt or suspicion.

CHARADES: (1) Parlor game devised by women to fend off men (1900-1909); (2) acting up in a skittish manner about the facts of life, instead of getting right down to them; twitching, nervous twitching.

COMPLEX: Mental crack-up caused by an emotional, or physical, inability to get away from, or wind things up with, a person of the opposite sex.

COMPLEX, NUCLEAR: Shock caused by discovery of a person of the opposite sex in his or her true colors; beginning of a general breakdown.

DEFENSE: Feminine excuses, tricks, devices, etc.

DELAY MECHANISM: Pother.

DETERIORATION (BENIGN): Going quietly to pieces as the result of marriage or a love affair.

DETERIORATION (MALIGNANT): Going loudly to pieces under the same circumstances; fidgeting, bawling, berating, etc.

DIVERSION SUBTERFUGE: Trick employed by women to keep men's minds on ethereal, rather than physical, matters.

EMPIRIC: National viewpoint of sex.

EROTIC: Of or pertaining to sex, usually in a pretty far-fetched manner.

EXHIBITIONISM: Going too far, but not really meaning it.

EXOTIC: Of an alarming nature, particularly to parents.

FIXATION: Too great dependence on one woman.

FRAGMENTATION OF PERSONALITY: Inception of general decline on the part of the male.

FRIGIDITY (in men): Suspicion, ignorance, or fatigue, mostly suspicion.

FUDGE-MAKING: Feminine trick or device.

FULLER'S RETORT: A remark made by a Paterson, N. J., girl one night in Paterson, N. J.

GEORGE SMITH: A despondent Indianapolis real-estate man. Pulling a George Smith: attempting to find something more important than, and just as interesting as, women.

JULIA MARLOWE: Actress.

LIBIDO: "Pleasure-principle."

LOOSENESS OF SYSTEMATIZATION: The going to pieces of a husband.

LOVE: The pleasant confusion which we know exists.

LOVING: Being confused by, or confusing some one.

MASCULINE PROTEST: Male disdain for things which he does not understand.

NARCISSISM: Attempt to be self-sufficient, with overtones.

NEURO-VEGETATIVE REFLEXES: A male's, particularly a husband's, quick, unpremeditated reactions to stewed vegetables, especially spinach, and to certain salads.

NEUROSIS: The beginning of the end, unless the husband can go away somewhere.

NEUROTIC: Wanting something, but she doesn't know what; desirous of something she hasn't got and probably can't, or shouldn't, have.

1907, PANIC OF: Result of woman's inhumanity to man (1900-1907).

NO BETTER THAN SHE OUGHT TO BE (woman's definitions): (1) indiscreet; (2) charming; (3) pretty and vivacious; (4) oversexed; (5) living in sin.

NORM: All Quiet.

NUMERICAL PROTECTION: Other people in the room.

OSCULATORY JUSTIFICATION: Reasons for kissing, growing out of the early American credo that kissing for kissing's sake would send one straight to hell.

PARANOIA: The last stages of what was once a bridegroom.

PASSION: Expression of the sex principle without so much fuss.

PEDESTALISM: The American male's reverence for the female or, better yet, her insistence on being revered, which amounts to the same thing.

PHYSICO-PSYCHIC: State in which the physical gets tangled up with the spiritual, after the manner of a setter pup throwing a huntsman by getting between his feet.

PLEASURE-PRINCIPLE: See Libido.

**POSSESSIVE COMPLEX:** Innocent desire to kiss and fondle, sometimes to maul or wool.

**POTHER:** Uncalled-for interest in something—almost always sex.

**PROTECTIVE REACTION:** Putting a man in his place.

**PSYCHE:** Wings for the feet of clay.

**PSYCHO-NEUROSIS:** Same as neurosis, only worse.

**PSYCHOSIS:** State of being beside oneself to such an extent that it is doubtful if one can pull oneself together.

**PULLED-AWAY:** Refers to the knee of a man who is suspicious or tired.

**RECESSIVE KNEE:** The outstanding phenomenon of masculine frigidity; man's refusal to answer the pressure.

**SCHMALHAUSEN, SAMUEL D.:** Student of misbehavior.

**SCHMALHAUSEN TROUBLE:** Illness commonly found in young ladies who read in cramped quarters.

**SMITH, GEORGE:** Same as George Smith.

**SWASTIKA:** Symbol which distracted American suitors used to scrawl on desk pads, margins of books, and so on.

**TROUBLE, SCHMALHAUSEN:** See Schmalhausen trouble.

**ÜBERTRAGUNG:** Period of transition during which the male strives to transmute his ardor for women into the semblance of ardor for games.

**VOYEURISM:** Sex Kibitzing.

# A NOTE ON THE DRAWINGS
# IN THIS BOOK

The inclusion, in this volume, of some fifty-two drawings by James Thurber, was on the whole intentional. Because, however, of the strong feeling of suspicion which they will arouse in certain quarters, it may not be amiss to offer some explanation. For this task I feel peculiarly fitted, for it was I who, during those trying months when the book was in the making, picked up the drawings night after night from the floor under Thurber's desk, picked them up when I was so tired in body and soul that I could scarcely stoop; it was I who, by gaining the confidence of the charwomen, nightly redeemed countless other thousands of unfinished sketches from the huge waste baskets; and finally, it was my incredible willingness to go through with the business of "inking-in" the drawings (necessitated by the fact that they were done in such faint strokes of a broken pencil as to be almost invisible to the naked eye) that at last brought them to the point where they could be engraved and reproduced.

To understand, even vaguely, Thurber's art, it is necessary to grasp the two major themes which underlie all his drawings. The first theme is what I call the "melancholy of sex"; the other is what I can best describe as the "implausibility of animals." These two basic ideas motivate, subconsciously, his entire creative life. Just how some of the animals shown in these pages "come in" is not clear even to me—except in so far as any animal must be regarded as sexually relevant because of our human tendency to overestimate what can be learned from watching it.

When one studies the drawings, it soon becomes apparent that a strong undercurrent of grief runs through them. In almost every instance the *man* in the picture is badly frightened, or even hurt. These "Thurber men" have come to be recognized as a distinct type in the world of art; they are frustrated, fugitive beings; at times they seem vaguely striving to get out of something without being seen (a room, a situation, a state of mind), at other times they are merely perplexed and too humble, or weak, to move. The *women*, you will notice, are quite different: temperamentally they are much better adjusted to their surroundings than are the men, and mentally they are much less capable of making themselves uncomfortable.

It would be foolish to attempt here a comprehensive appreciation of the fierce sweep, the economy, and the magnificent obscurity of Thurber's work, nor can I adequately indicate the stark qualities in the drawings that have earned for him the title of "the Ugly Artist." All I, all anybody, can do is to hint at the uncanny faithfulness with which he has caught—caught and thrown to the floor —the daily, indeed the almost momently, severity of life's mystery, as well as the charming doubtfulness of its purpose.

E.B.W.

# BOOKS BY THE AUTHORS

**IS SEX NECESSARY?:** *Or Why You Feel the Way You Do*
ISBN 0-06-073314-4 (paperback)      JAMES THURBER AND E. B. WHITE

A masterful comic foray into the mysteries of romance, love, and marriage featuring
fifty-two of Thurber's incomparably funny drawings.

**THE DOG DEPARTMENT**
*James Thurber on Hounds, Scotties, and Talking Poodles*
ISBN 0-06-019656-4 (hardcover)      JAMES THURBER AND MICHAEL J. ROSEN

Thurber's best prose and drawings from *Thurber's Dogs*, along with unpublished
material and a large selection of "Talk of the Town" miniatures.

**FABLES FOR OUR TIME**
ISBN 0-06-090999-4 (paperback)      JAMES THURBER

Here are a score or more lessons-in-prose dedicated to conventional sinners and
supplemented by Mr. Thurber's own pictorial interpretations.

**MY LIFE AND HARD TIMES**
ISBN 0-06-093308-9 (paperback)      JAMES THURBER

Thurber looks back at his own life of delightful chaos and the frustrations of family,
boyhood, odd dogs, recalcitrant machinery, and the foibles of human nature.

**THE THURBER CARNIVAL**
ISBN 0-06-093287-2 (paperback)      JAMES THURBER

Including selections from such beloved classics as *My World and Welcome to It*,
*The Owl in the Attic*, *The Seal in the Bathroom*, and *Men, Women and Dogs*.

**THE YEARS WITH ROSS**
ISBN 0-06-095971-1 (paperback)      JAMES THURBER

A memoir of Thurber's time at *The New Yorker* with editor Harold Ross—at once
an informal biography, a history of the magazine, and a recounting of friendship.

**ESSAYS OF E. B. WHITE**
ISBN 0-06-093223-6 (paperback)      E. B. WHITE

A classic collection of writings by one of the greatest essayists of our time.

**WRITINGS FROM THE NEW YORKER 1925–1976**
ISBN 0-06-092123-4 (paperback)      E. B. WHITE

A delightful, witty, spirited collection of short pieces and essays.